# FOREGONE IN INCREDIBLE HERCULES

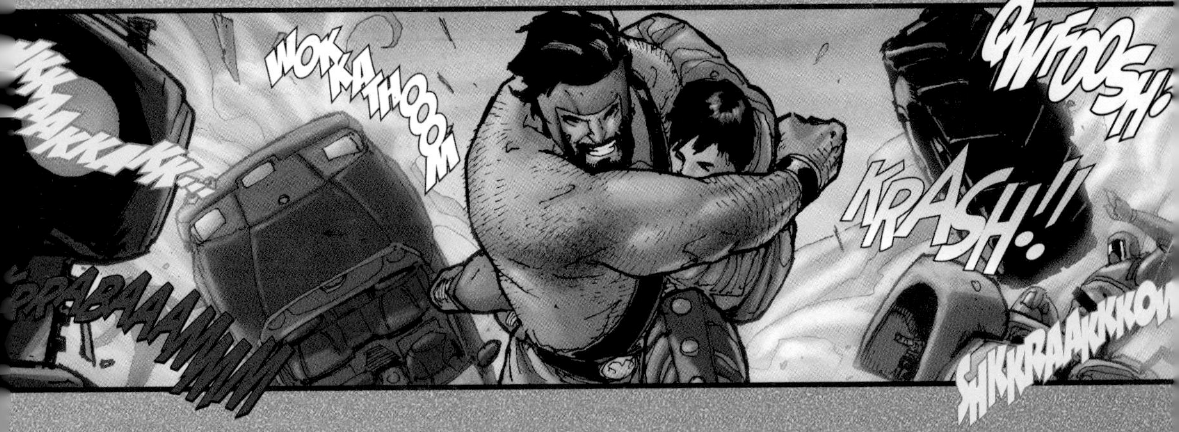
WOKKATHOOOM
KRASH!!
SHKKRAAKKOW

YON HERCULES AND CHO HAVE JOURNEYED FAR.

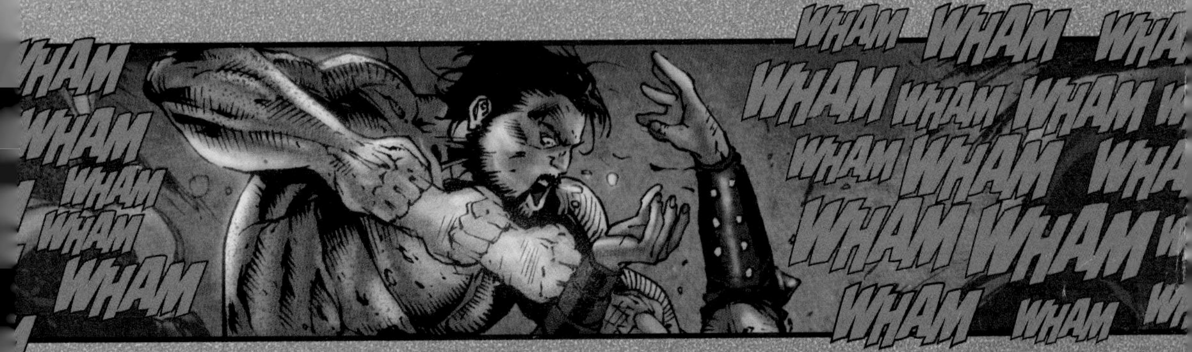
WHAM WHAM WHAM
WHAM WHAM WHAM
WHAM WHAM WHAM
WHAM WHAM
WHAM WHAM

THERE HAS BEEN MUCH BASHING THRASHING CRASHING LASHING MASHING GNASHING DASHING TRASHING GASHING AND CLASHING.

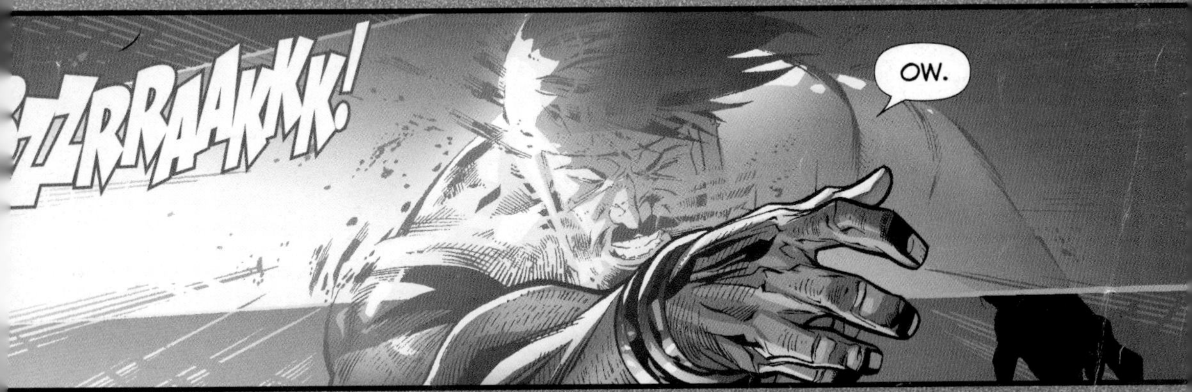
OW.

THE TIME IS RIPE FOR A CHILL-OUT, YO.
(E'EN GODS NEED A HOLIDAY)

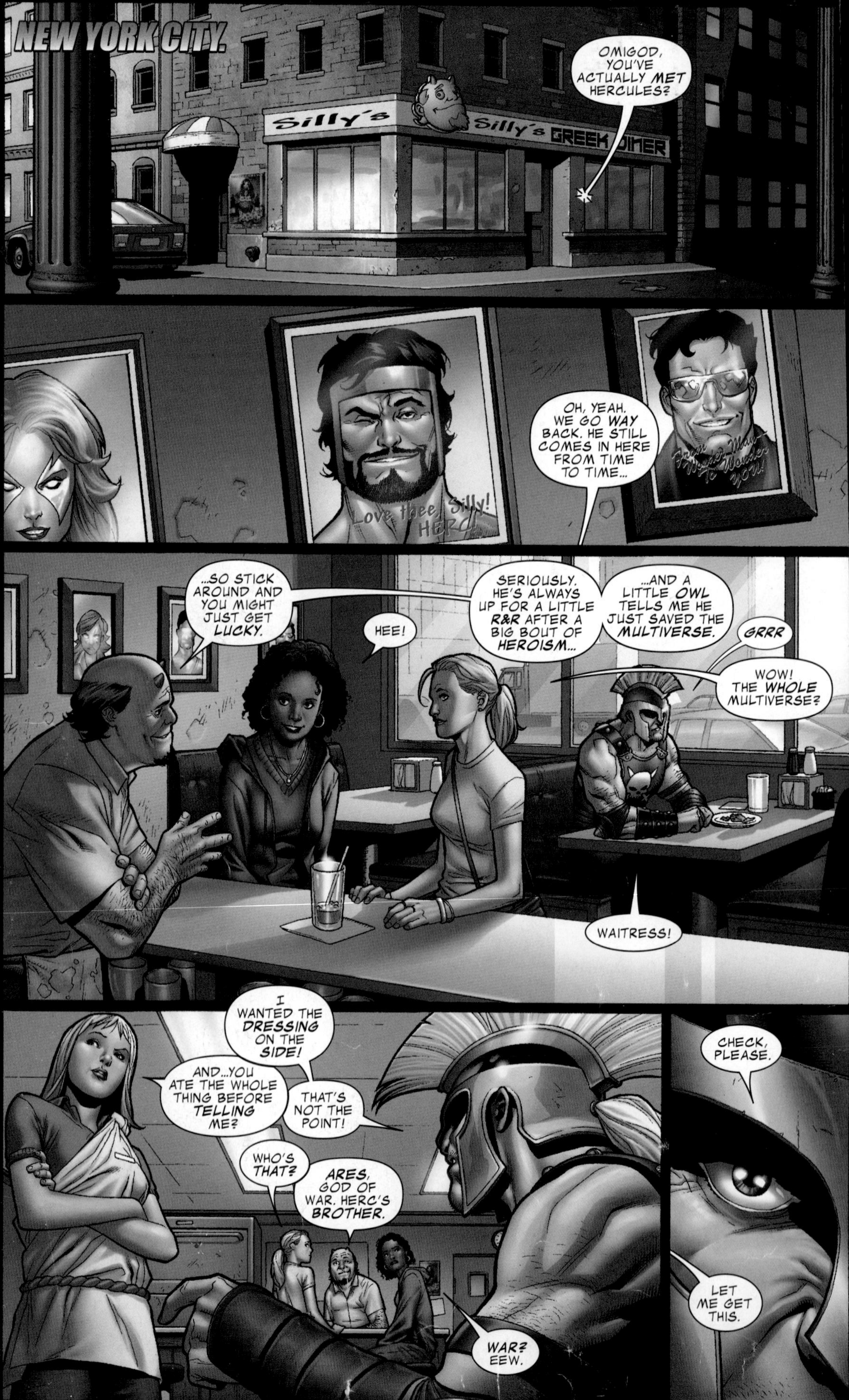
NEW YORK CITY.
Silly's
Silly's GREEK DINER
OMIGOD, YOU'VE ACTUALLY MET HERCULES?
OH, YEAH. WE GO WAY BACK. HE STILL COMES IN HERE FROM TIME TO TIME...
Love thee, Silly! HERC!
...SO STICK AROUND AND YOU MIGHT JUST GET LUCKY.
HEE!
SERIOUSLY. HE'S ALWAYS UP FOR A LITTLE R&R AFTER A BIG BOUT OF HEROISM...
...AND A LITTLE OWL TELLS ME HE JUST SAVED THE MULTIVERSE.
GRRR
WOW! THE WHOLE MULTIVERSE?
WAITRESS!
I WANTED THE DRESSING ON THE SIDE!
AND...YOU ATE THE WHOLE THING BEFORE TELLING ME?
THAT'S NOT THE POINT!
WHO'S THAT?
ARES, GOD OF WAR. HERC'S BROTHER.
WAR? EEW.
CHECK, PLEASE.
LET ME GET THIS.

# THE INCREDIBLE HERCULES

Writers: **GREG PAK** & **FRED VAN LENTE**

Artists: **CLAYTON HENRY** & **SALVA ESPIN**

Colorists: **GURU EFX, RAÚL TREVIÑO** & **LEE LOUGHRIDGE**

Letterers: **VIRTUAL CALLIGRAPHY'S JOE CARAMAGNA** & **CHRIS ELIOPOULOS**

Cover Artists: **ARTHUR SUYDAM, CLAY HENRY** & **GURU EFX,**

**BOB LAYTON** & **GURU EFX AND ED MCGUINNESS** & **GURU EFX**

Assistant Editors: **NATHAN COSBY** & **JORDAN D. WHITE**

Editor: **MARK PANICCIA**

Collection Editor: **CORY LEVINE**

Editorial Assistant: **ALEX STARBUCK**

Assistant Editor: **JOHN DENNING**

Editors, Special Projects: **JENNIFER GRÜNWALD** & **MARK D. BEAZLEY**

Senior Editor, Special Projects: **JEFF YOUNGQUIST**

Senior Vice President of Sales: **DAVID GABRIEL**

Production: **CARRIE BEADLE**

Editor in Chief: **JOE QUESADA**

Publisher: **DAN BUCKLEY**

INCREDIBLE HERCULES: LOVE AND WAR. Contains material originally published in magazine form as INCREDIBLE HERCULES #121-125. First printing 2009. Hardcover ISBN# 978-0-7851-3334-6. Softcover ISBN# 978-0-7851-3246-2. Published by MARVEL PUBLISHING, INC., a subsidiary of MARVEL ENTERTAINMENT, INC. OFFICE OF PUBLICATION: 417 5th Avenue, New York, NY 10016. Copyright © 2008 and 2009 Marvel Characters, Inc. All rights reserved. Hardcover: $19.99 per copy in the U.S. (GST #R127032852). Softcover: $14.99 per copy in the U.S. (GST #R127032852). Canadian Agreement #40668537. All characters featured in this issue and the distinctive names and likenesses thereof, and all related indicia are trademarks of Marvel Characters, Inc. No similarity between any of the names, characters, persons, and/or institutions in this magazine with those of any living or dead person or institution is intended, and any such similarity which may exist is purely coincidental. **Printed in the U.S.A.** ALAN FINE, CEO Marvel Toys & Publishing Divisions and CMO Marvel Characters, Inc.; JIM SOKOLOWSKI, Chief Operating Officer; DAVID GABRIEL, SVP of Publishing Sales & Circulation; DAVID BOGART, SVP of Business Affairs & Talent Management; MICHAEL PASCIULLO, VP Merchandising & Communications; JIM O'KEEFE, VP of Operations & Logistics; DAN CARR, Executive Director of Publishing Technology; JUSTIN F. GABRIE, Director of Publishing & Editorial Operations; SUSAN CRESPI, Editorial Operations Manager; ALEX MORALES, Publishing Operations Manager; STAN LEE, Chairman Emeritus. For information regarding advertising in Marvel Comics or on Marvel.com, please contact Mitch Dane, Advertising Director, at mdane@marvel.com. For Marvel subscription inquiries, please call 800-217-9158.

10 9 8 7 6 5 4 3 2 1

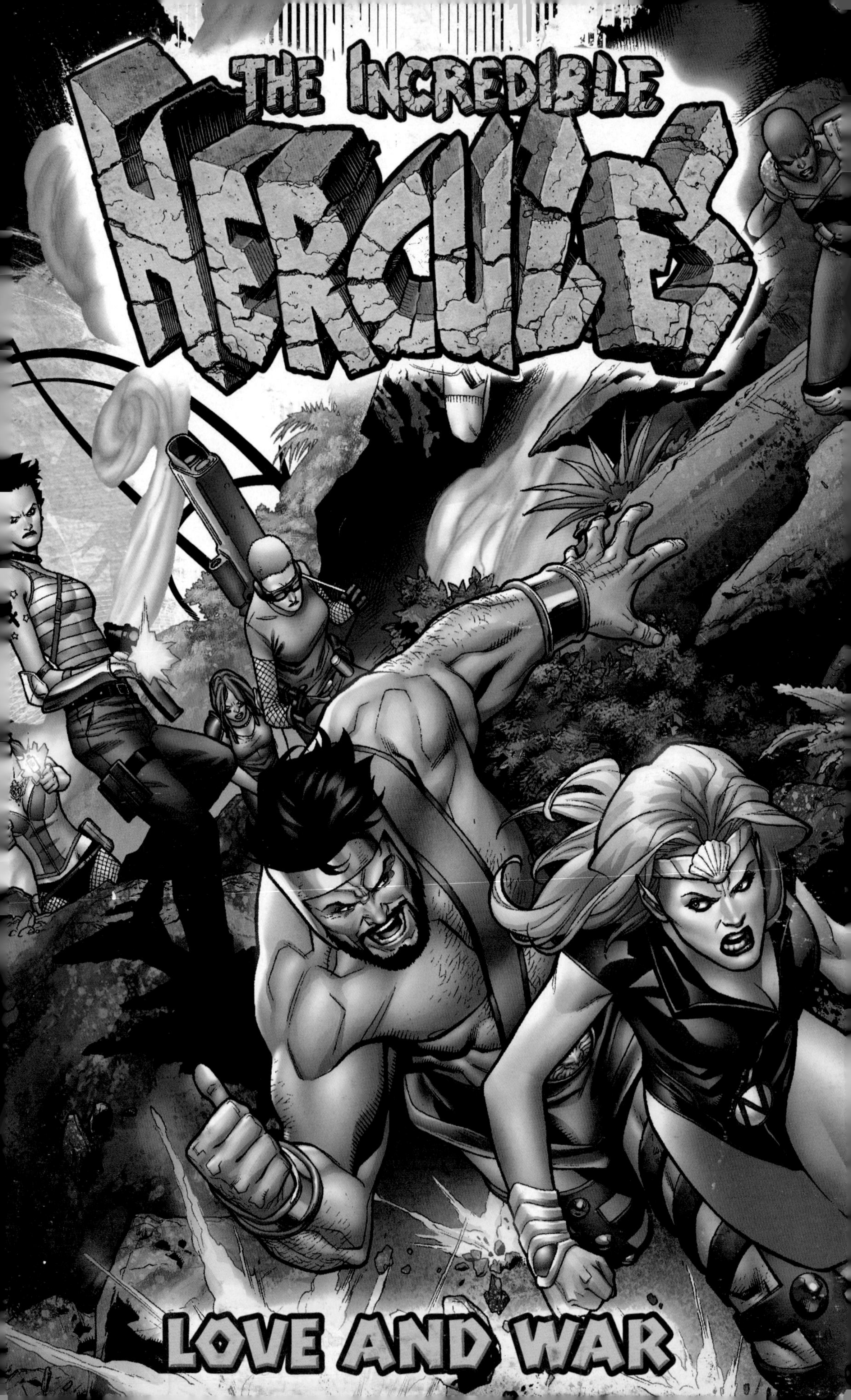
THE INCREDIBLE
HERCULES
LOVE AND WAR

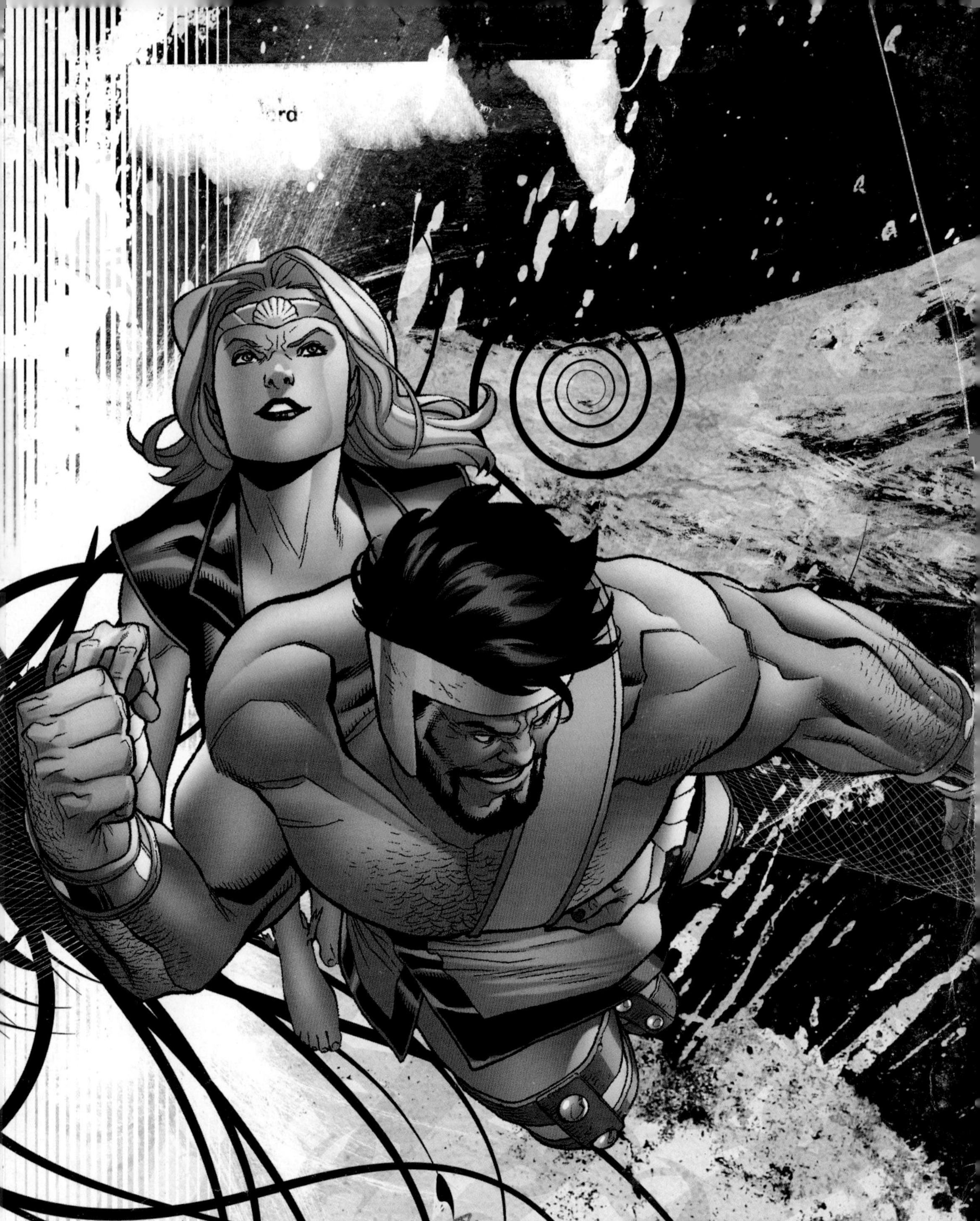

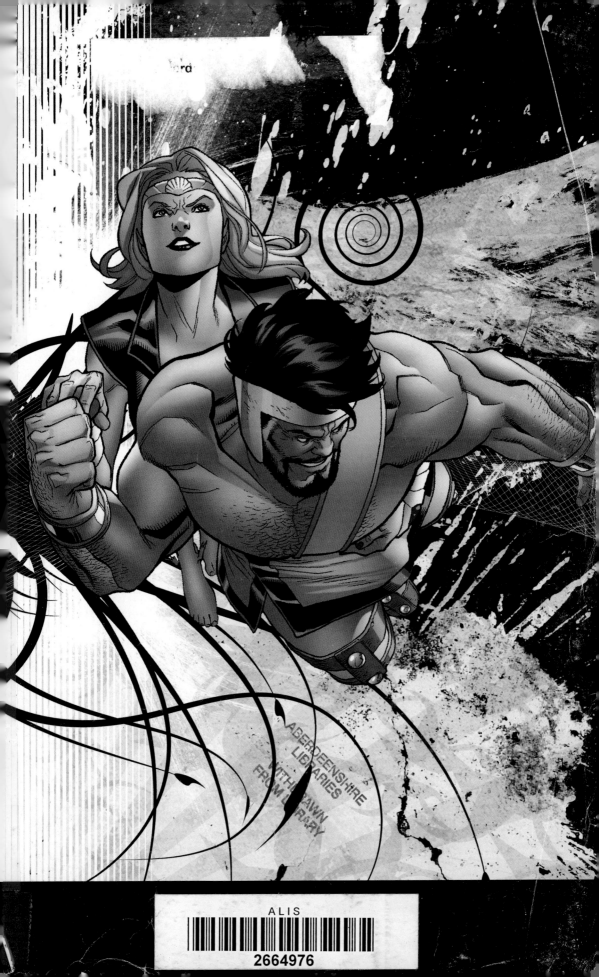

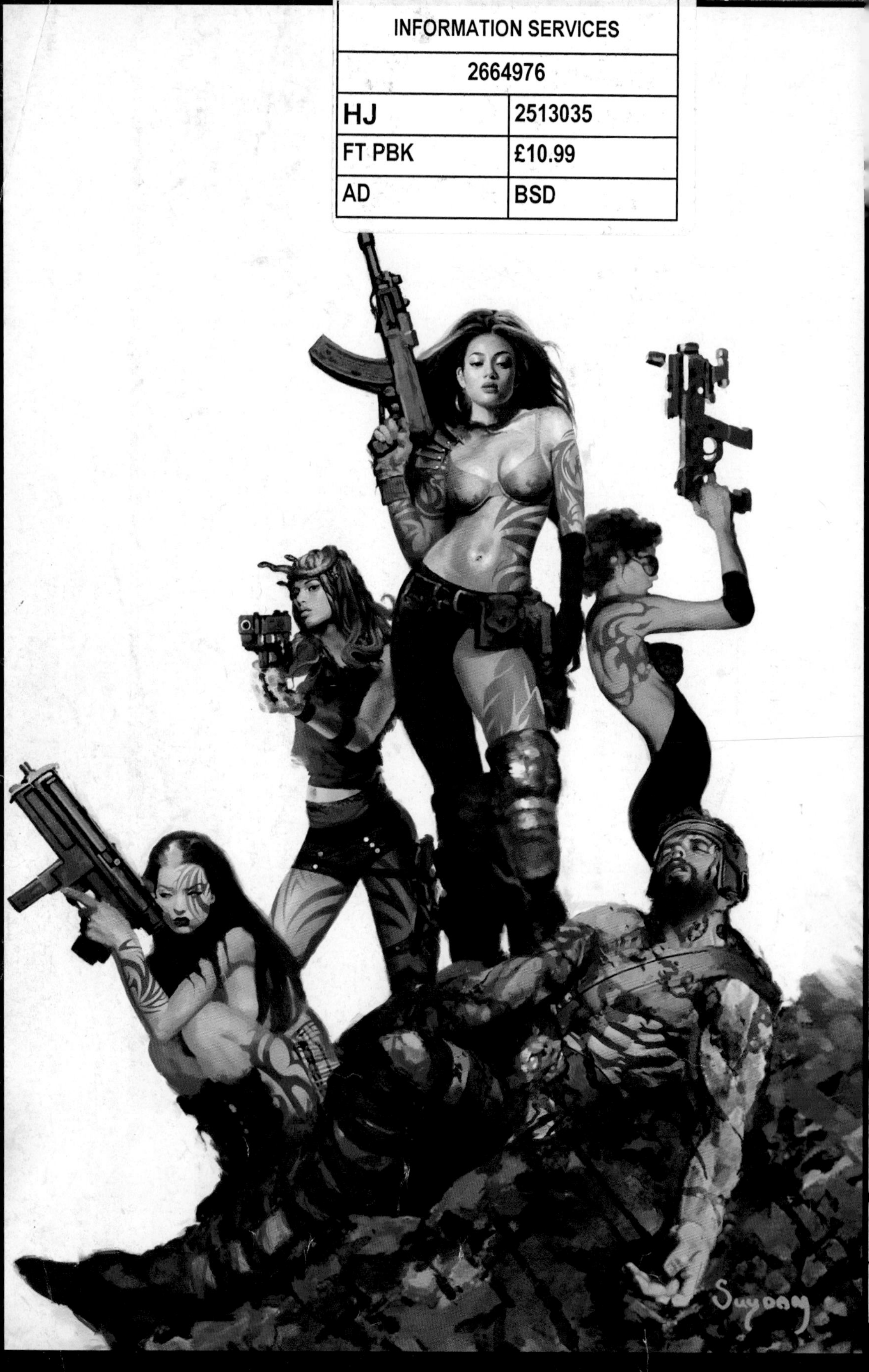

INCREDIBLE HERCULES #121

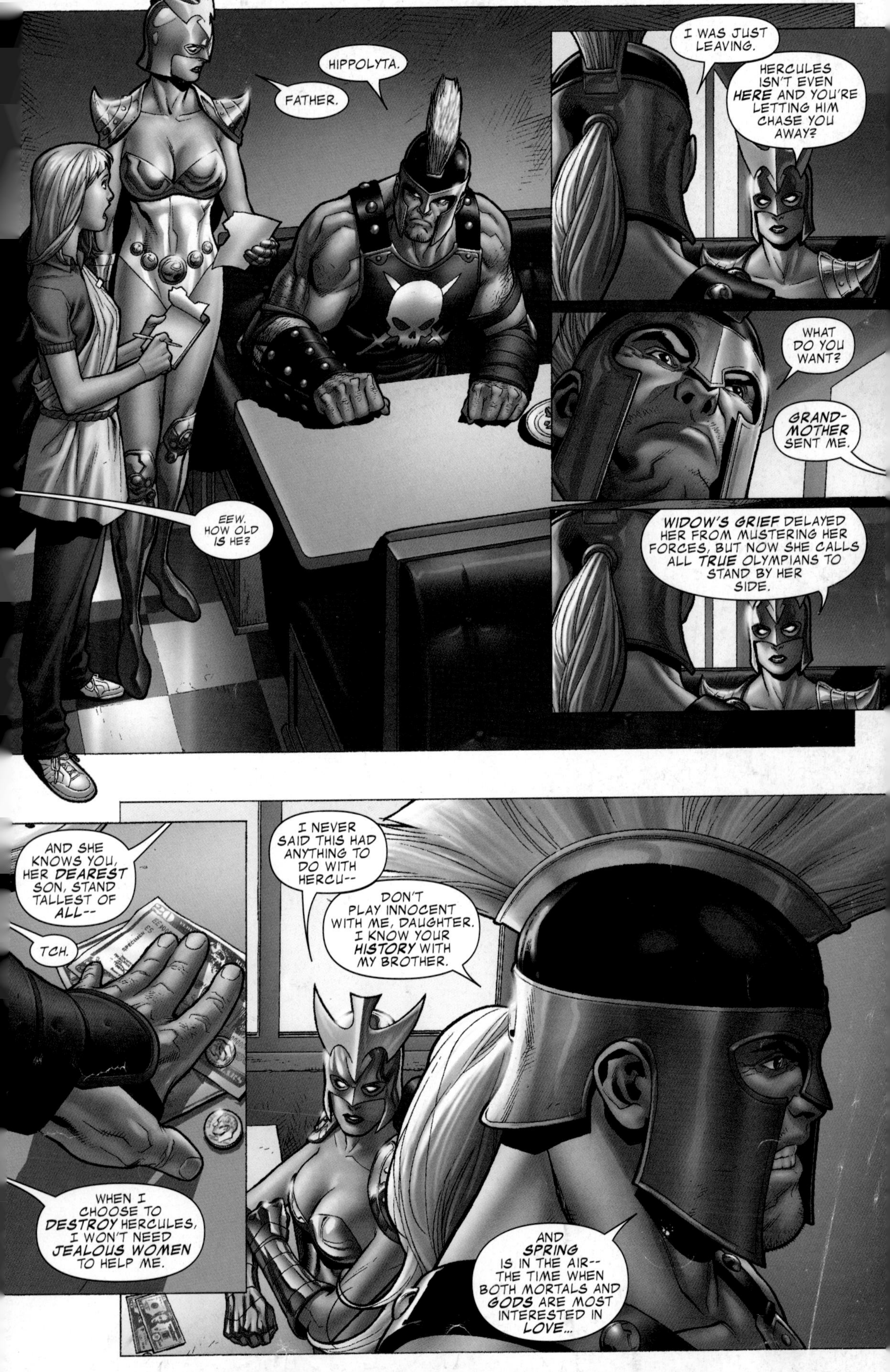
HIPPOLYTA.
FATHER.
EEW. HOW OLD IS HE?
I WAS JUST LEAVING.
HERCULES ISN'T EVEN HERE AND YOU'RE LETTING HIM CHASE YOU AWAY?
WHAT DO YOU WANT?
GRAND-MOTHER SENT ME.
WIDOW'S GRIEF DELAYED HER FROM MUSTERING HER FORCES, BUT NOW SHE CALLS ALL TRUE OLYMPIANS TO STAND BY HER SIDE.
AND SHE KNOWS YOU, HER DEAREST SON, STAND TALLEST OF ALL--
TCH.
I NEVER SAID THIS HAD ANYTHING TO DO WITH HERCU--
DON'T PLAY INNOCENT WITH ME, DAUGHTER. I KNOW YOUR HISTORY WITH MY BROTHER.
WHEN I CHOOSE TO DESTROY HERCULES, I WON'T NEED JEALOUS WOMEN TO HELP ME.
AND SPRING IS IN THE AIR-- THE TIME WHEN BOTH MORTALS AND GODS ARE MOST INTERESTED IN LOVE...

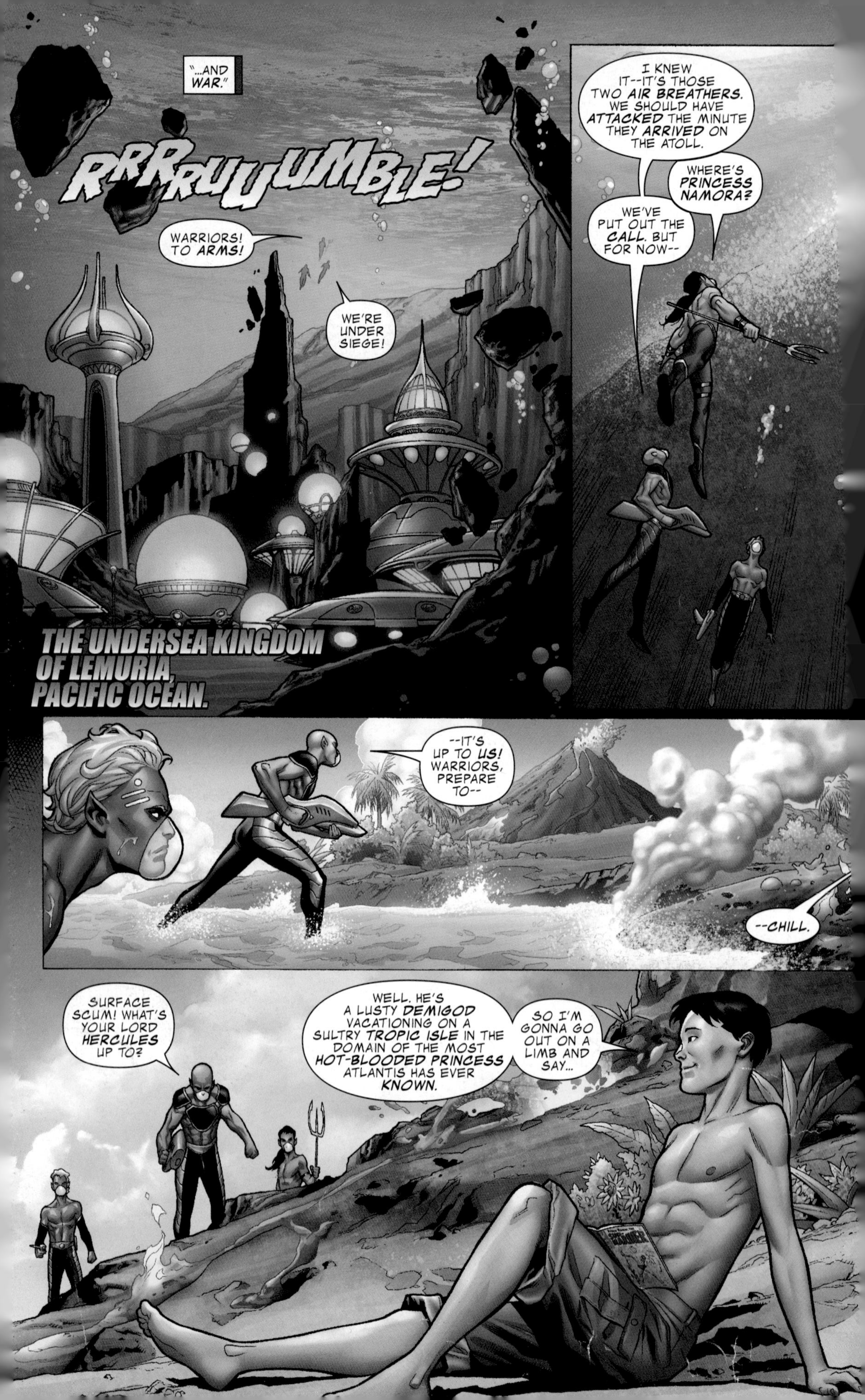

"...AND WAR."
RRRRUUUUMBLE!
WARRIORS! TO ARMS!
WE'RE UNDER SIEGE!
THE UNDERSEA KINGDOM OF LEMURIA, PACIFIC OCEAN.
I KNEW IT--IT'S THOSE TWO AIR BREATHERS. WE SHOULD HAVE ATTACKED THE MINUTE THEY ARRIVED ON THE ATOLL.
WHERE'S PRINCESS NAMORA?
WE'VE PUT OUT THE CALL. BUT FOR NOW--
--IT'S UP TO US! WARRIORS, PREPARE TO--
--CHILL.
SURFACE SCUM! WHAT'S YOUR LORD HERCULES UP TO?
WELL. HE'S A LUSTY DEMIGOD VACATIONING ON A SULTRY TROPIC ISLE IN THE DOMAIN OF THE MOST HOT-BLOODED PRINCESS ATLANTIS HAS EVER KNOWN.
SO I'M GONNA GO OUT ON A LIMB AND SAY...

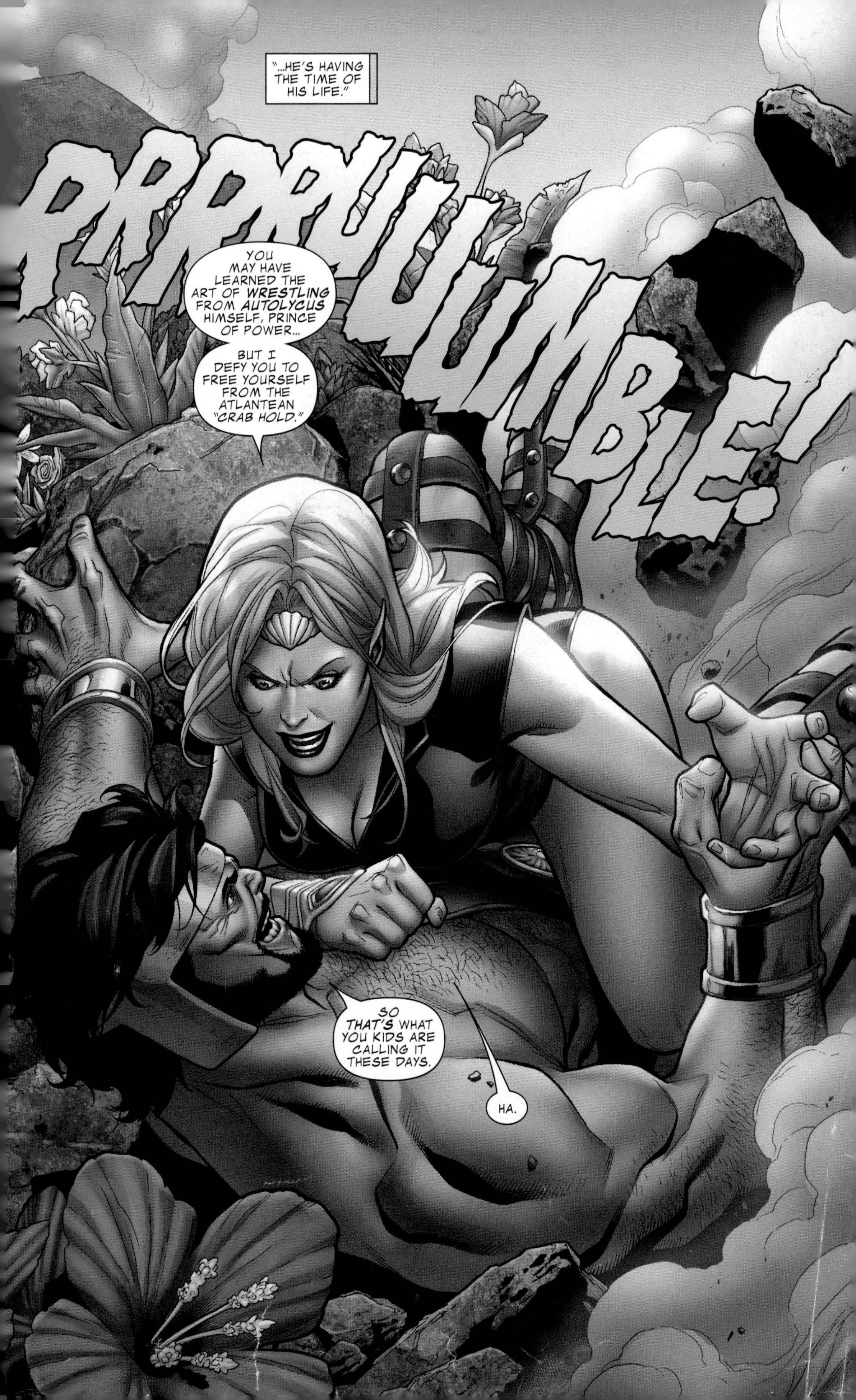
"...HE'S HAVING THE TIME OF HIS LIFE."
PRRRUUUMBLE!!
YOU MAY HAVE LEARNED THE ART OF WRESTLING FROM AUTOLYCUS HIMSELF, PRINCE OF POWER...
BUT I DEFY YOU TO FREE YOURSELF FROM THE ATLANTEAN "CRAB HOLD."
SO THAT'S WHAT YOU KIDS ARE CALLING IT THESE DAYS.
HA.

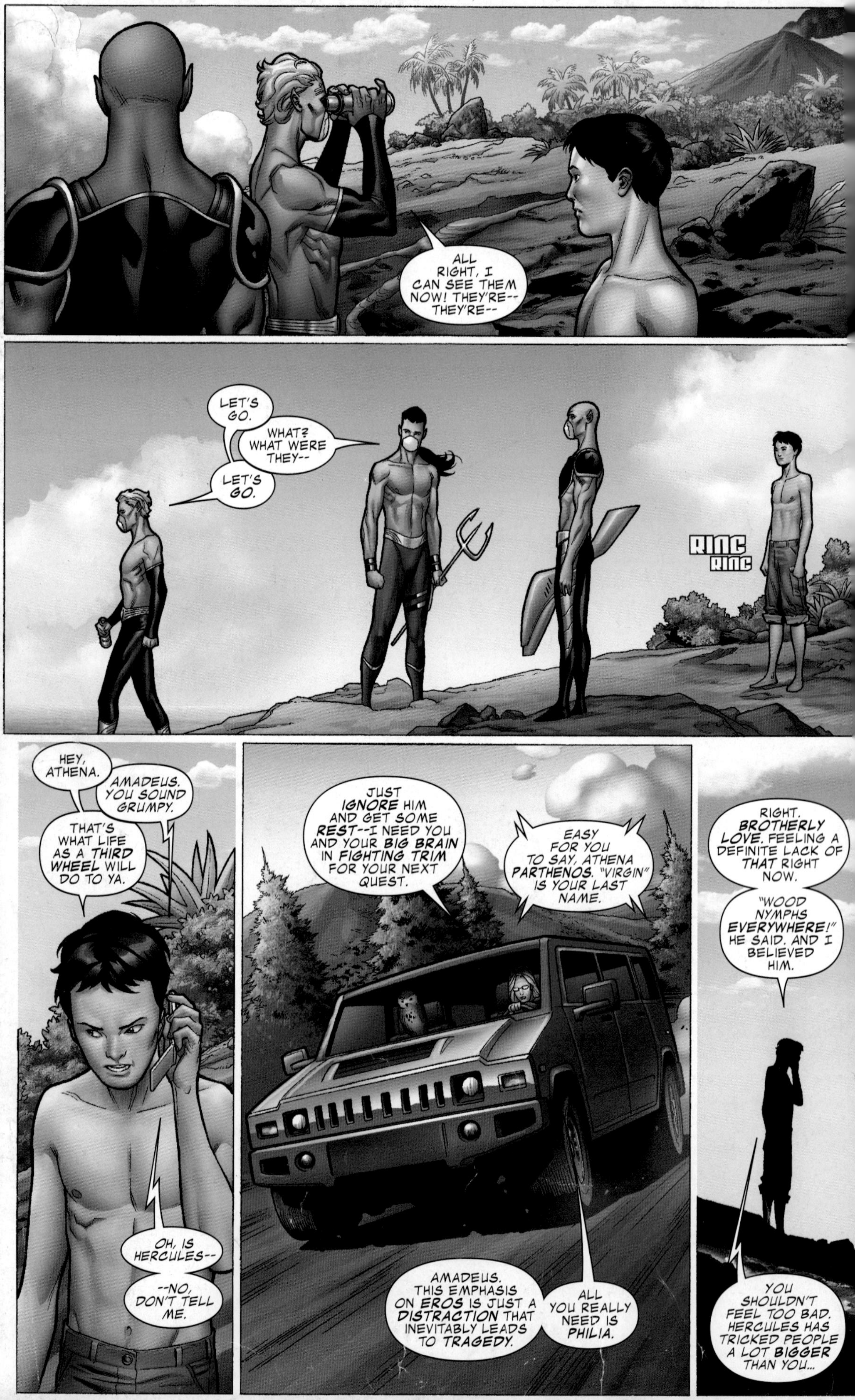
ALL RIGHT, I CAN SEE THEM NOW! THEY'RE-- THEY'RE--
LET'S GO.
WHAT? WHAT WERE THEY--
LET'S GO.
RING RING
HEY, ATHENA.
AMADEUS. YOU SOUND GRUMPY.
THAT'S WHAT LIFE AS A THIRD WHEEL WILL DO TO YA.
OH, IS HERCULES--
--NO, DON'T TELL ME.
JUST IGNORE HIM AND GET SOME REST--I NEED YOU AND YOUR BIG BRAIN IN FIGHTING TRIM FOR YOUR NEXT QUEST.
EASY FOR YOU TO SAY, ATHENA PARTHENOS. "VIRGIN" IS YOUR LAST NAME.
AMADEUS. THIS EMPHASIS ON EROS IS JUST A DISTRACTION THAT INEVITABLY LEADS TO TRAGEDY.
ALL YOU REALLY NEED IS PHILIA.
RIGHT. BROTHERLY LOVE. FEELING A DEFINITE LACK OF THAT RIGHT NOW.
"WOOD NYMPHS EVERYWHERE!" HE SAID. AND I BELIEVED HIM.
YOU SHOULDN'T FEEL TOO BAD. HERCULES HAS TRICKED PEOPLE A LOT BIGGER THAN YOU...

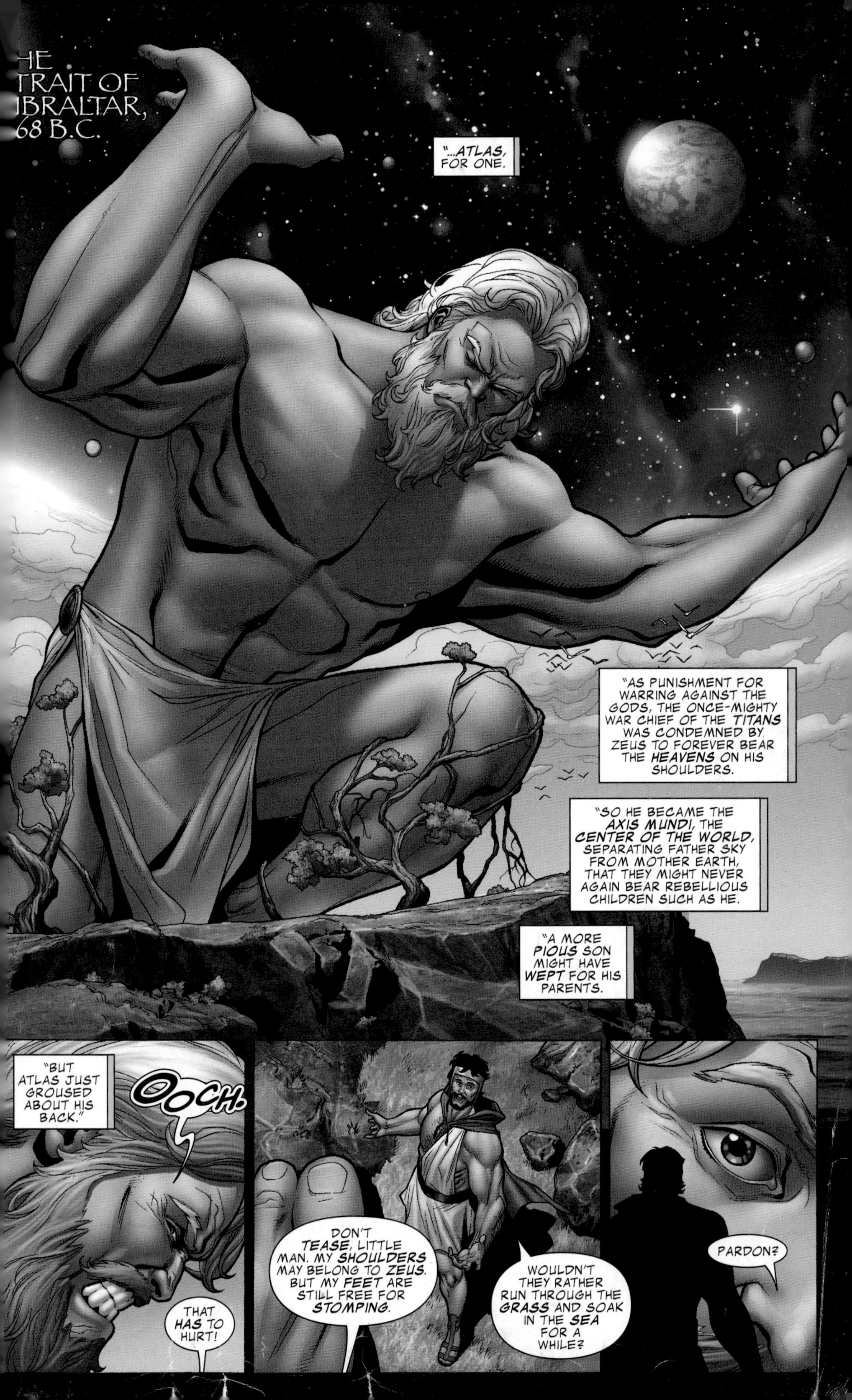

HE
TRAIT OF
IBRALTAR,
68 B.C.
"...ATLAS, FOR ONE.
"AS PUNISHMENT FOR WARRING AGAINST THE GODS, THE ONCE-MIGHTY WAR CHIEF OF THE TITANS WAS CONDEMNED BY ZEUS TO FOREVER BEAR THE HEAVENS ON HIS SHOULDERS.
"SO HE BECAME THE AXIS MUNDI, THE CENTER OF THE WORLD, SEPARATING FATHER SKY FROM MOTHER EARTH, THAT THEY MIGHT NEVER AGAIN BEAR REBELLIOUS CHILDREN SUCH AS HE.
"A MORE PIOUS SON MIGHT HAVE WEPT FOR HIS PARENTS.
"BUT ATLAS JUST GROUSED ABOUT HIS BACK."
OOCH.
THAT HAS TO HURT!
DON'T TEASE, LITTLE MAN. MY SHOULDERS MAY BELONG TO ZEUS. BUT MY FEET ARE STILL FREE FOR STOMPING.
WOULDN'T THEY RATHER RUN THROUGH THE GRASS AND SOAK IN THE SEA FOR A WHILE?
PARDON?

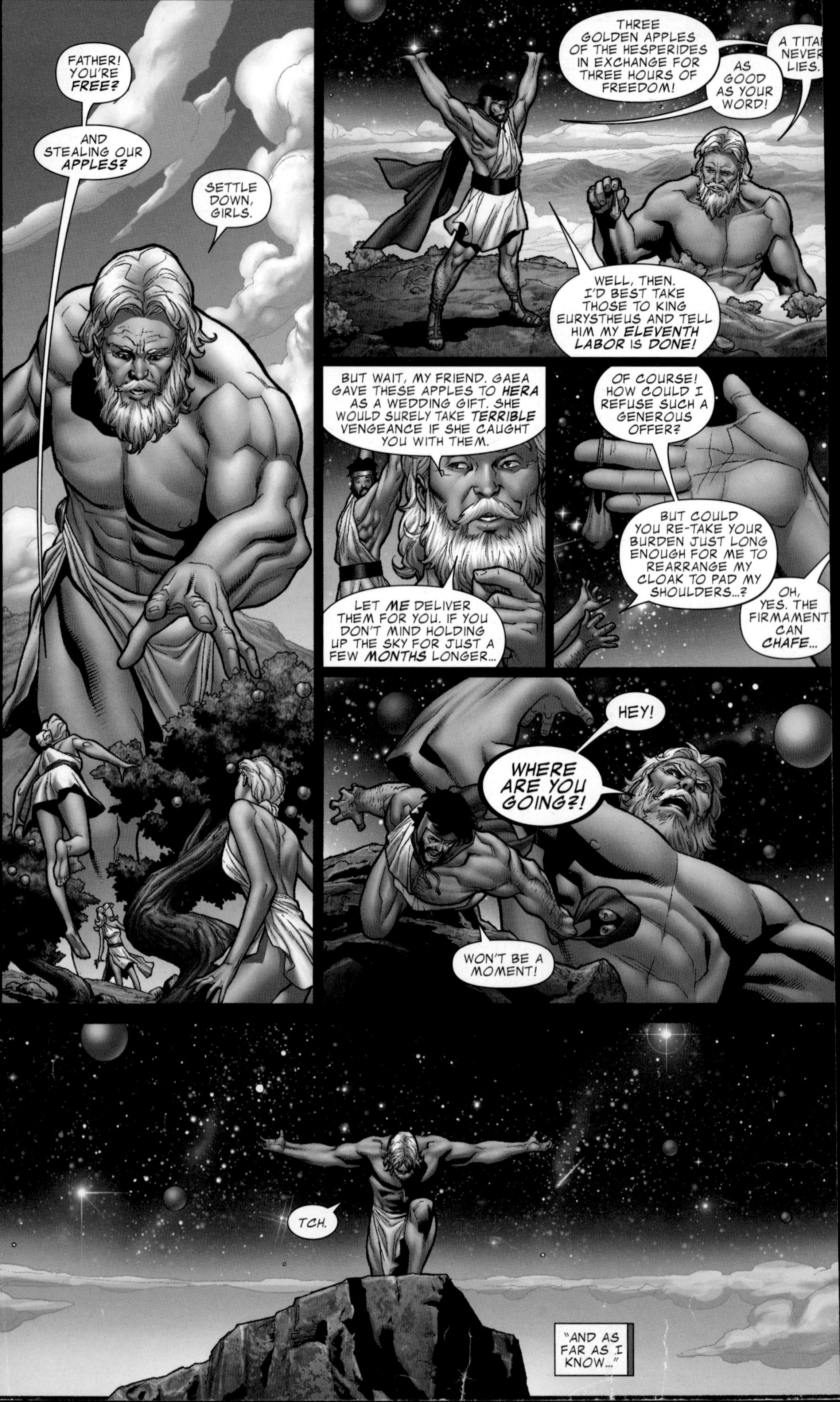
FATHER! YOU'RE FREE?
AND STEALING OUR APPLES?
SETTLE DOWN, GIRLS.
THREE GOLDEN APPLES OF THE HESPERIDES IN EXCHANGE FOR THREE HOURS OF FREEDOM!
AS GOOD AS YOUR WORD!
A TITAN NEVER LIES.
WELL, THEN. I'D BEST TAKE THOSE TO KING EURYSTHEUS AND TELL HIM MY ELEVENTH LABOR IS DONE!
BUT WAIT, MY FRIEND. GAEA GAVE THESE APPLES TO HERA AS A WEDDING GIFT. SHE WOULD SURELY TAKE TERRIBLE VENGEANCE IF SHE CAUGHT YOU WITH THEM.
LET ME DELIVER THEM FOR YOU. IF YOU DON'T MIND HOLDING UP THE SKY FOR JUST A FEW MONTHS LONGER...
OF COURSE! HOW COULD I REFUSE SUCH A GENEROUS OFFER?
BUT COULD YOU RE-TAKE YOUR BURDEN JUST LONG ENOUGH FOR ME TO REARRANGE MY CLOAK TO PAD MY SHOULDERS...?
OH, YES. THE FIRMAMENT CAN CHAFE...
HEY!
WHERE ARE YOU GOING?!
WON'T BE A MOMENT!
TCH.
"AND AS FAR AS I KNOW..."

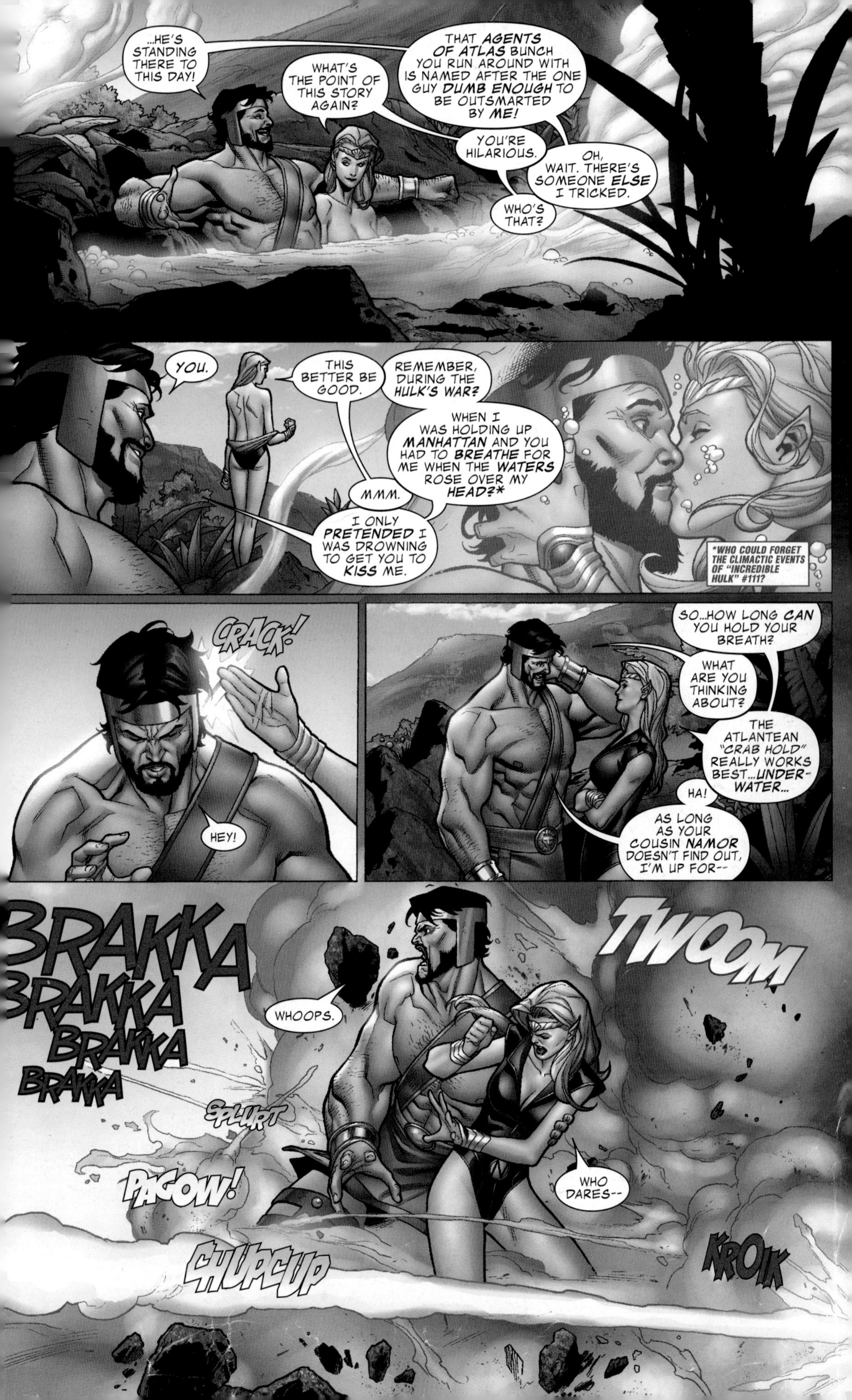

...HE'S STANDING THERE TO THIS DAY!
THAT AGENTS OF ATLAS BUNCH YOU RUN AROUND WITH IS NAMED AFTER THE ONE GUY DUMB ENOUGH TO BE OUTSMARTED BY ME!
WHAT'S THE POINT OF THIS STORY AGAIN?
YOU'RE HILARIOUS.
OH, WAIT. THERE'S SOMEONE ELSE I TRICKED.
WHO'S THAT?
YOU.
THIS BETTER BE GOOD.
REMEMBER, DURING THE HULK'S WAR?
WHEN I WAS HOLDING UP MANHATTAN AND YOU HAD TO BREATHE FOR ME WHEN THE WATERS ROSE OVER MY HEAD?*
MMM.
I ONLY PRETENDED I WAS DROWNING TO GET YOU TO KISS ME.
*WHO COULD FORGET THE CLIMACTIC EVENTS OF "INCREDIBLE HULK" #111?
CRACK!
HEY!
SO...HOW LONG CAN YOU HOLD YOUR BREATH?
WHAT ARE YOU THINKING ABOUT?
THE ATLANTEAN "CRAB HOLD" REALLY WORKS BEST...UNDER-WATER...
HA!
AS LONG AS YOUR COUSIN NAMOR DOESN'T FIND OUT, I'M UP FOR--
BRAKKA BRAKKA BRAKKA BRAKKA
TWOOM
WHOOPS.
SPLURT
PAGOW!
WHO DARES--
CHUPCUP
KROIK

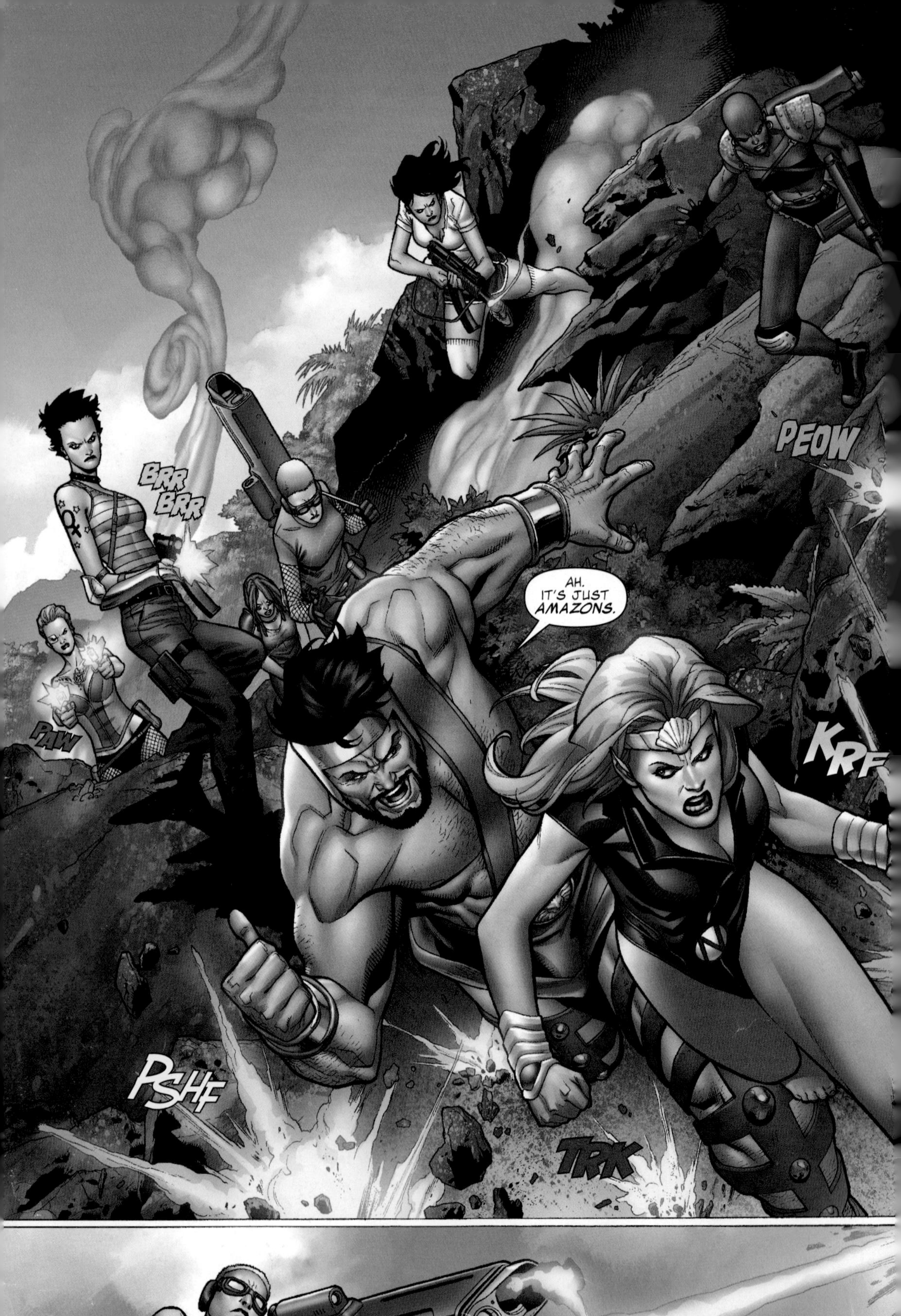
BRR BRR
PAW
PEOW
AH. IT'S JUST AMAZONS.
KRF
PSHF
TRK

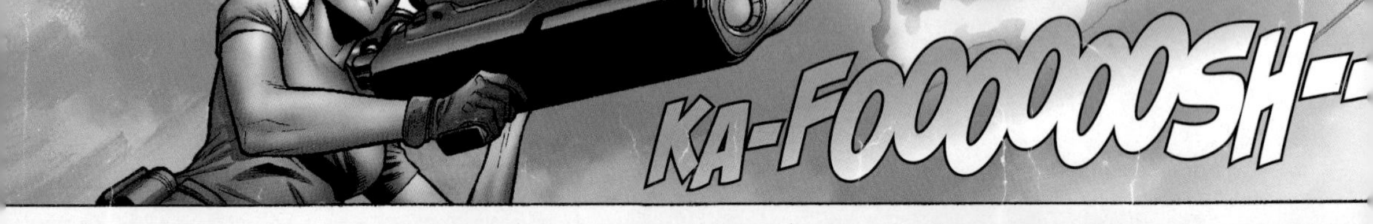
KA-FOOOOOOOSH--

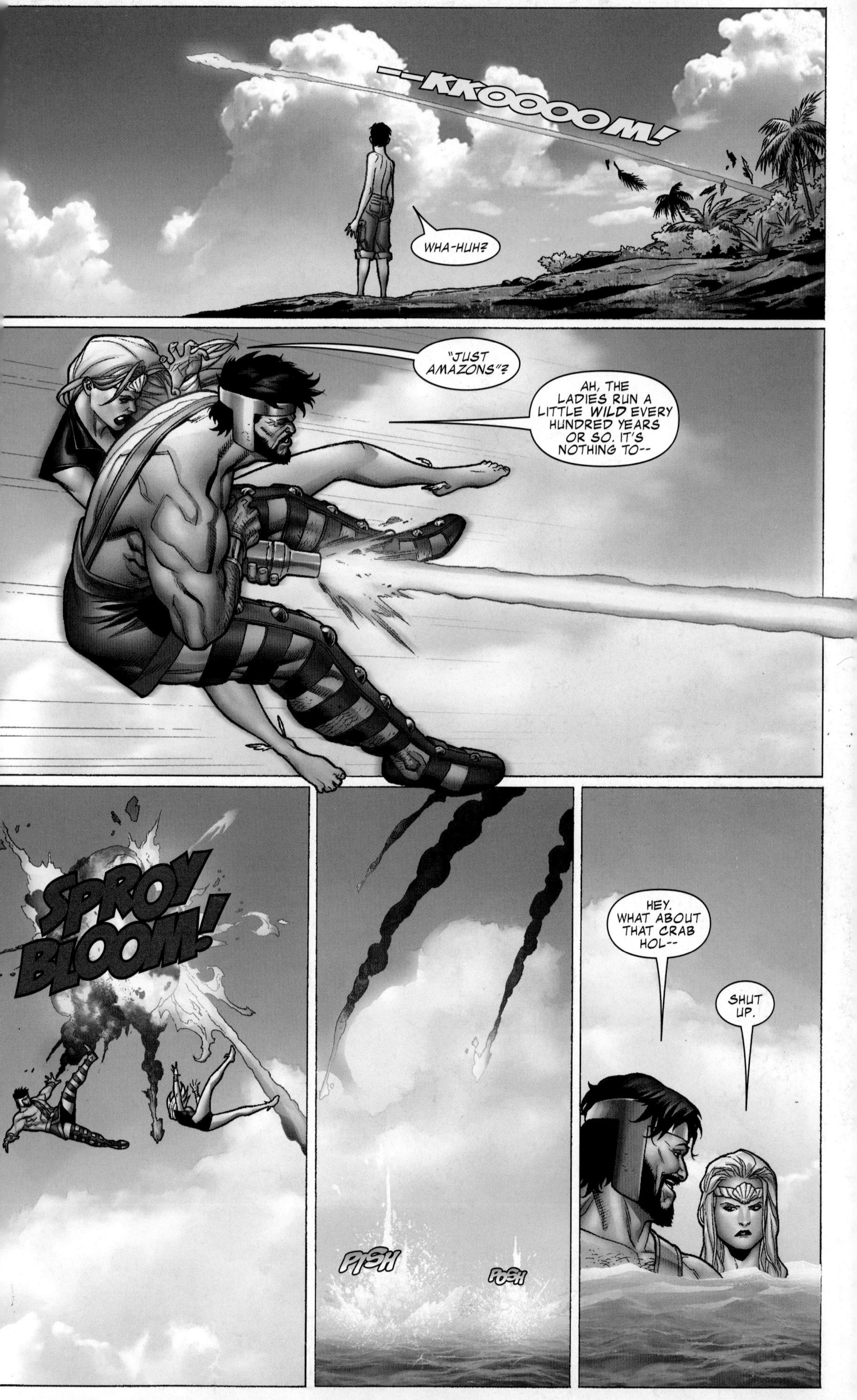
--KKOOOOOM!
WHA-HUH?
"JUST AMAZONS"?
AH, THE LADIES RUN A LITTLE WILD EVERY HUNDRED YEARS OR SO. IT'S NOTHING TO--
SPROY BLOOOM!
PTSH
POSH
HEY. WHAT ABOUT THAT CRAB HOL--
SHUT UP.

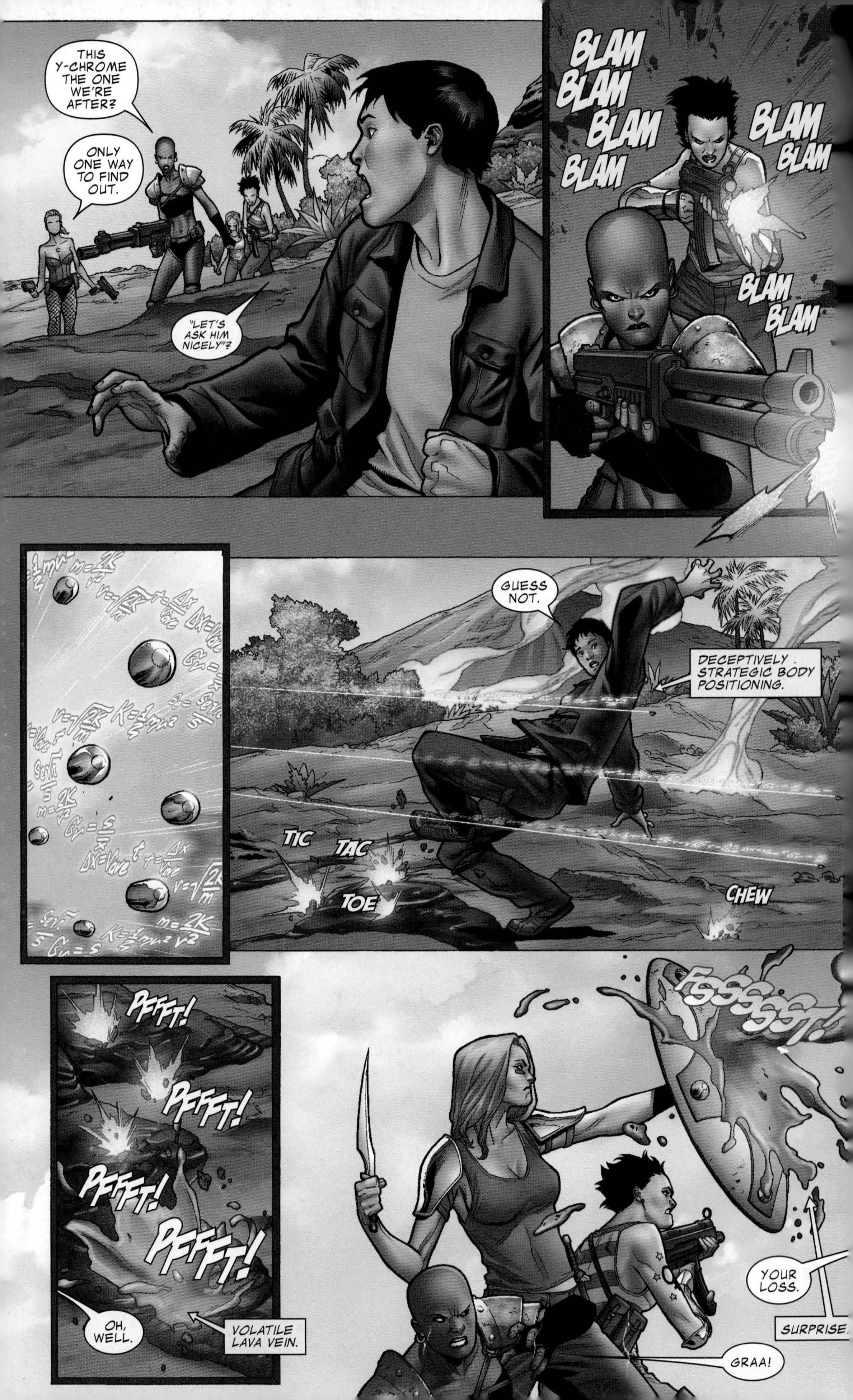
THIS Y-CHROME THE ONE WE'RE AFTER?
ONLY ONE WAY TO FIND OUT.
"LET'S ASK HIM NICELY"?
BLAM BLAM BLAM BLAM
BLAM BLAM
BLAM BLAM
GUESS NOT.
DECEPTIVELY STRATEGIC BODY POSITIONING.
TIC
TAC
TOE
CHEW
PFFFT!
PFFFT!
PFFFT!
PFFFT!
OH, WELL.
VOLATILE LAVA VEIN.
FSSSSST!
YOUR LOSS.
SURPRISE.
GRAA!

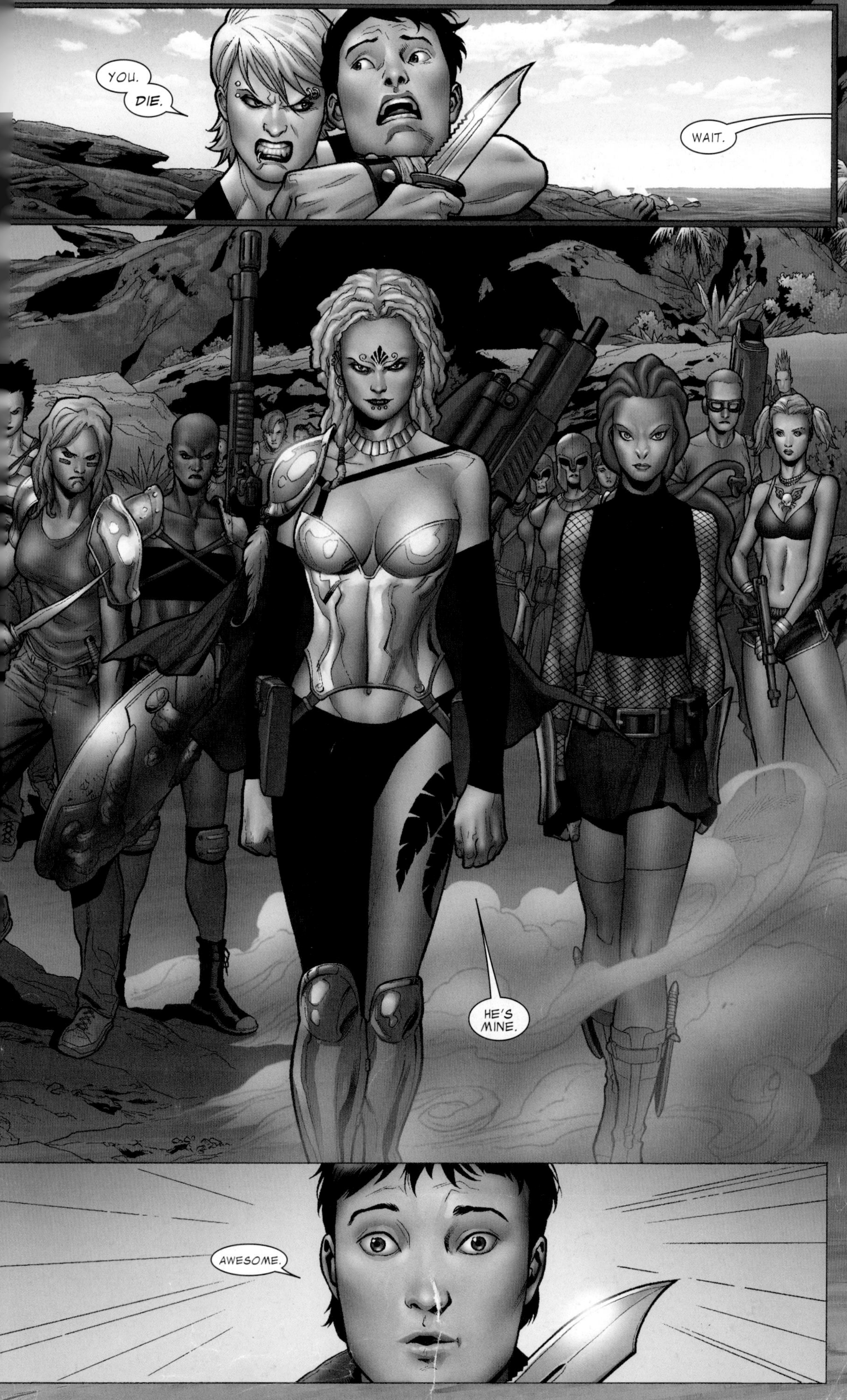
YOU.
DIE.
WAIT.
HE'S MINE.
AWESOME.

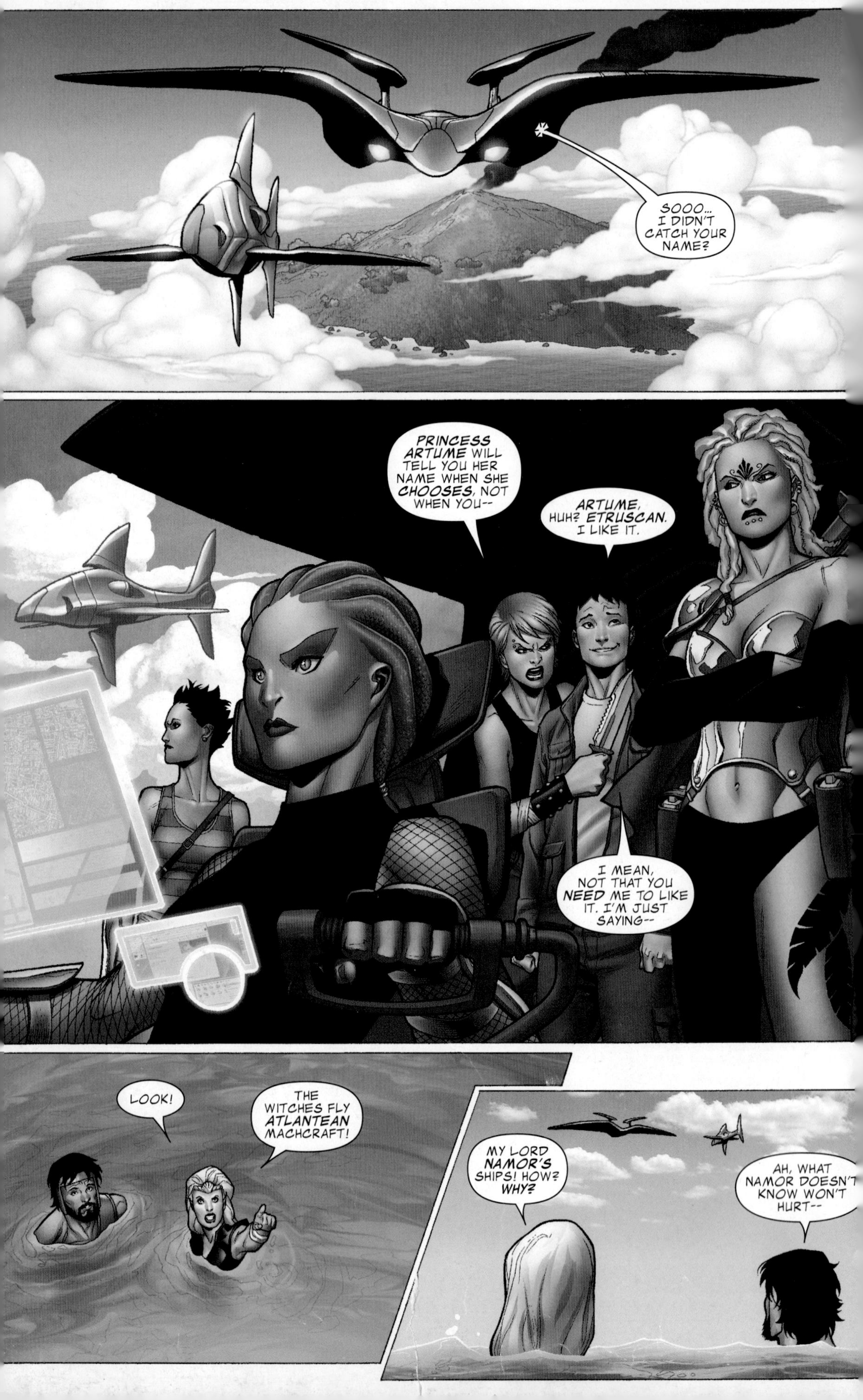
SOOO... I DIDN'T CATCH YOUR NAME?
PRINCESS ARTUME WILL TELL YOU HER NAME WHEN SHE CHOOSES, NOT WHEN YOU--
ARTUME, HUH? ETRUSCAN. I LIKE IT.
I MEAN, NOT THAT YOU NEED ME TO LIKE IT. I'M JUST SAYING--
LOOK!
THE WITCHES FLY ATLANTEAN MACHCRAFT!
MY LORD NAMOR'S SHIPS! HOW? WHY?
AH, WHAT NAMOR DOESN'T KNOW WON'T HURT--

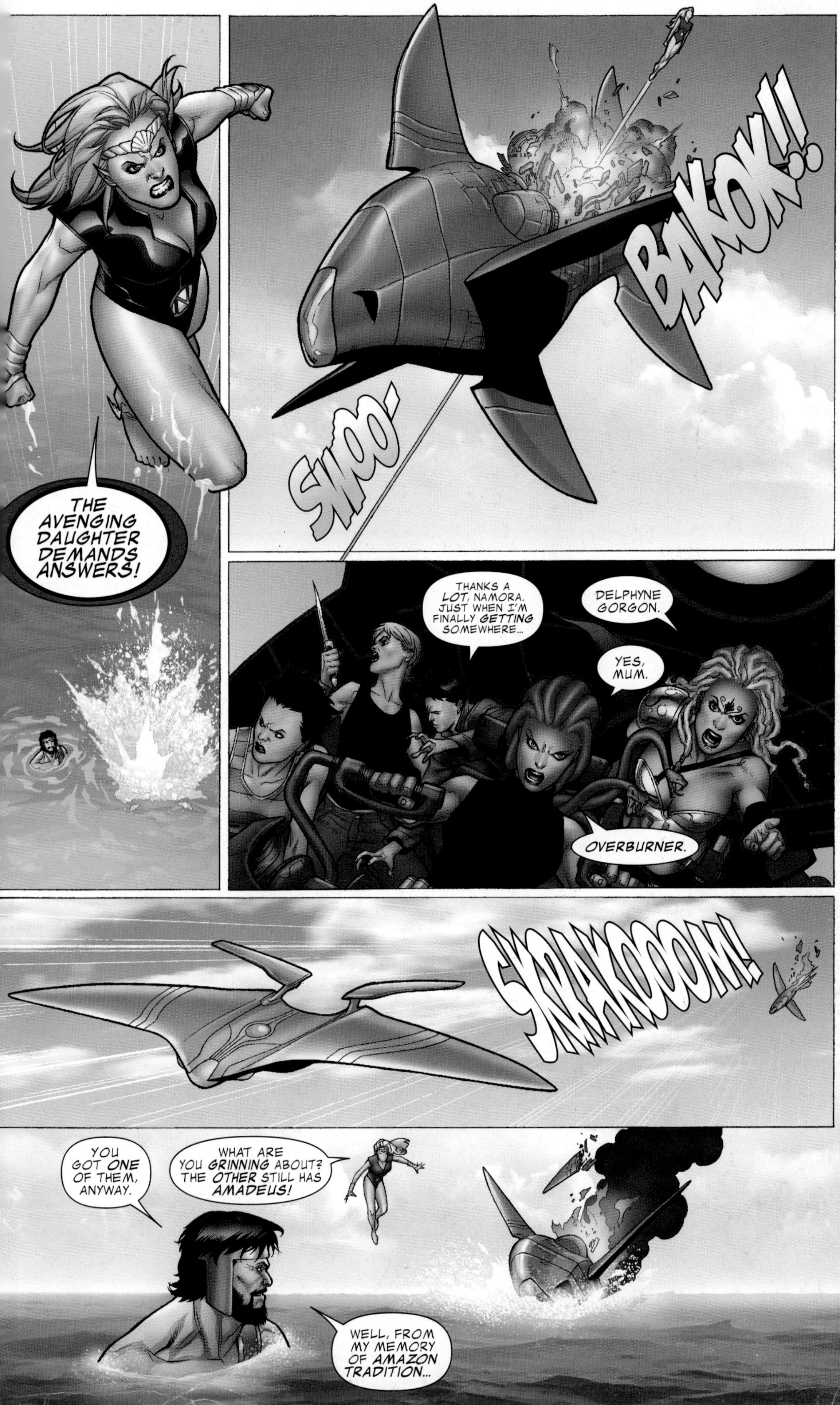
THE AVENGING DAUGHTER DEMANDS ANSWERS!
SWOO-
BAKOK!!
THANKS A LOT, NAMORA. JUST WHEN I'M FINALLY GETTING SOMEWHERE...
DELPHYNE GORGON.
YES, MUM.
OVERBURNER.
SKRAKOOOM!
YOU GOT ONE OF THEM, ANYWAY.
WHAT ARE YOU GRINNING ABOUT? THE OTHER STILL HAS AMADEUS!
WELL, FROM MY MEMORY OF AMAZON TRADITION...

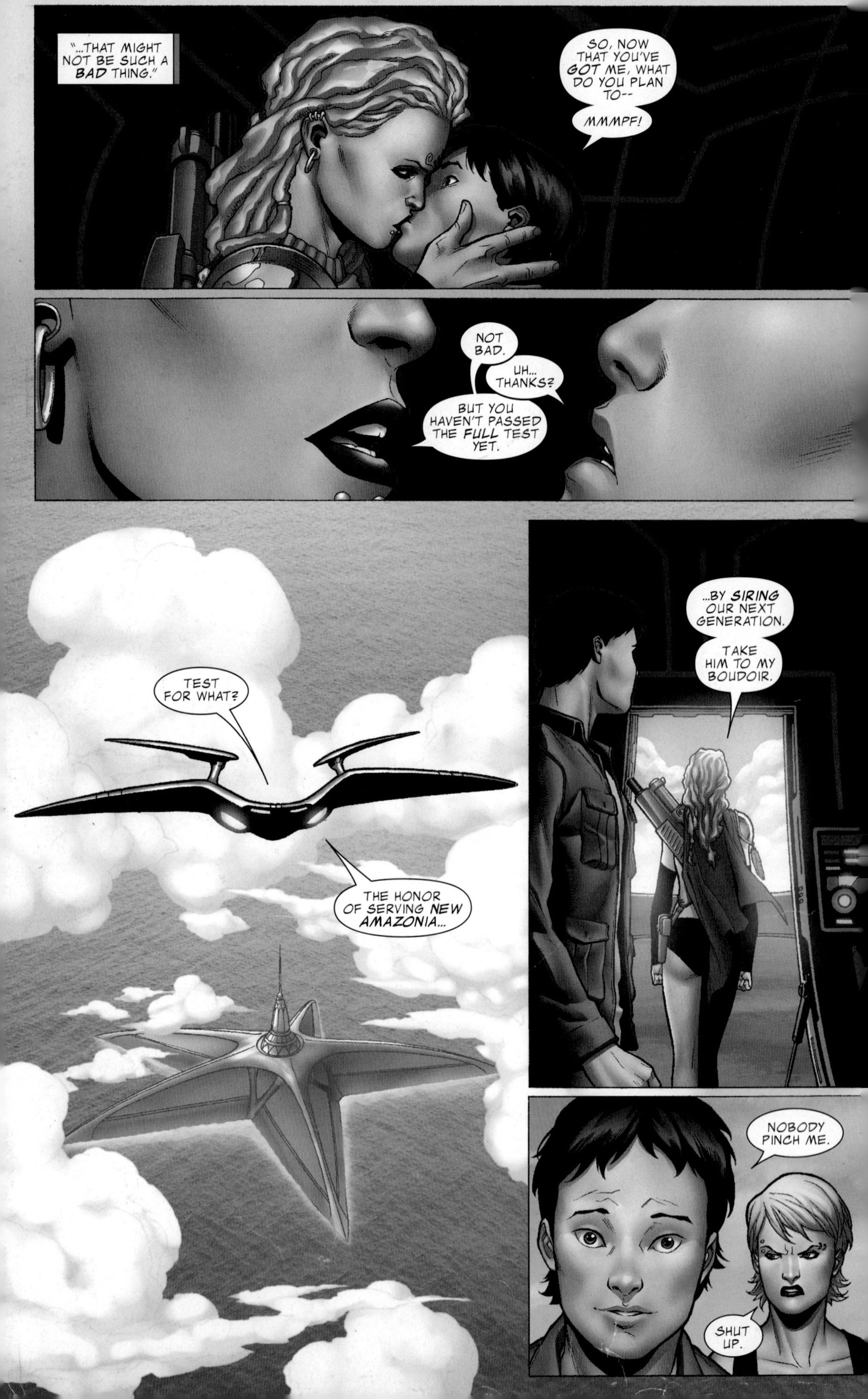
"...THAT MIGHT NOT BE SUCH A BAD THING."
SO, NOW THAT YOU'VE GOT ME, WHAT DO YOU PLAN TO--
MMMPF!
NOT BAD.
UH... THANKS?
BUT YOU HAVEN'T PASSED THE FULL TEST YET.
TEST FOR WHAT?
THE HONOR OF SERVING NEW AMAZONIA...
...BY SIRING OUR NEXT GENERATION.
TAKE HIM TO MY BOUDOIR.
NOBODY PINCH ME.
SHUT UP.

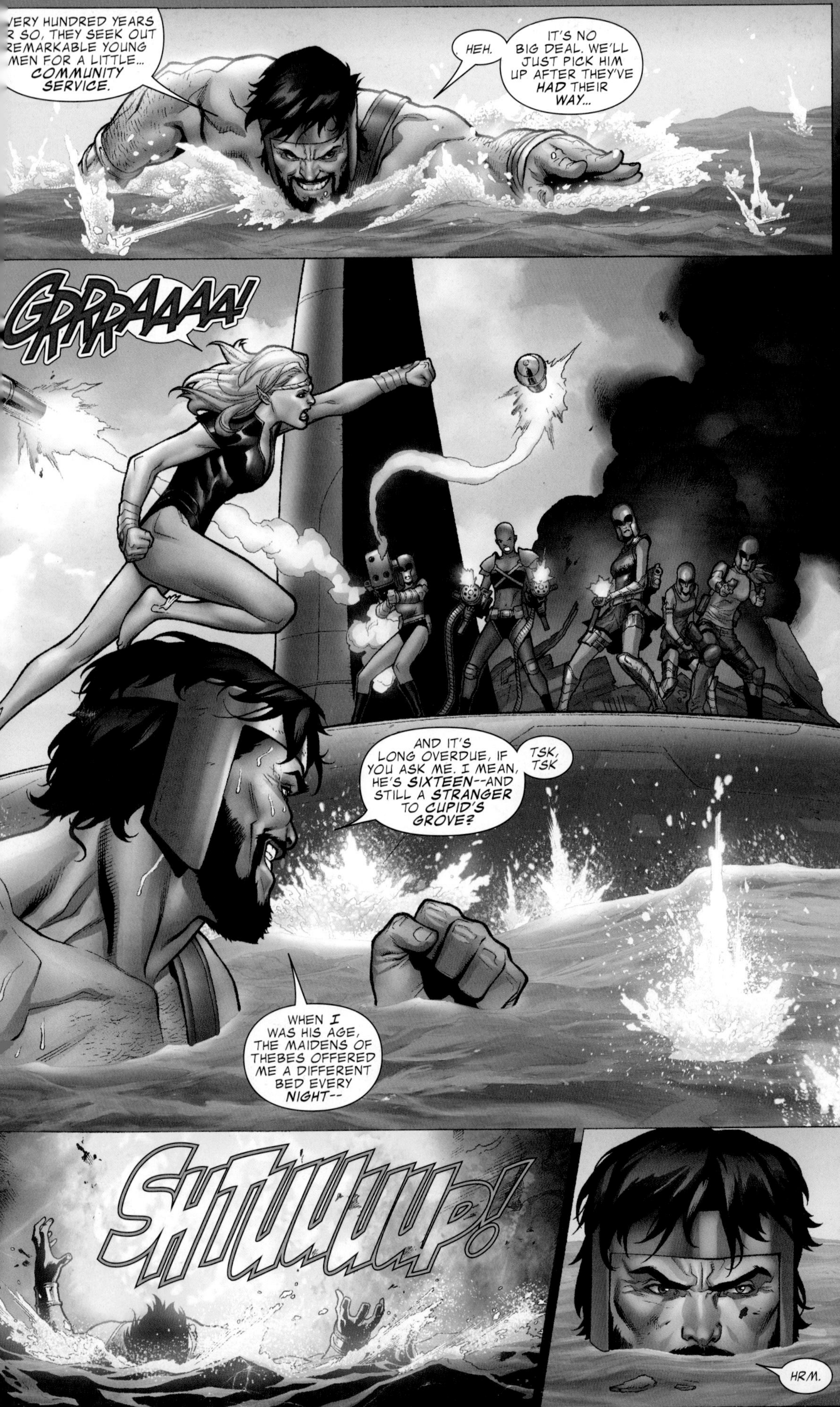
VERY HUNDRED YEARS R SO, THEY SEEK OUT REMARKABLE YOUNG MEN FOR A LITTLE... COMMUNITY SERVICE.
HEH.
IT'S NO BIG DEAL. WE'LL JUST PICK HIM UP AFTER THEY'VE HAD THEIR WAY...
GRRRAAAA!
AND IT'S LONG OVERDUE, IF YOU ASK ME. I MEAN, HE'S SIXTEEN--AND STILL A STRANGER TO CUPID'S GROVE?
TSK, TSK
WHEN I WAS HIS AGE, THE MAIDENS OF THEBES OFFERED ME A DIFFERENT BED EVERY NIGHT--
SHUUUUP!
HRM.

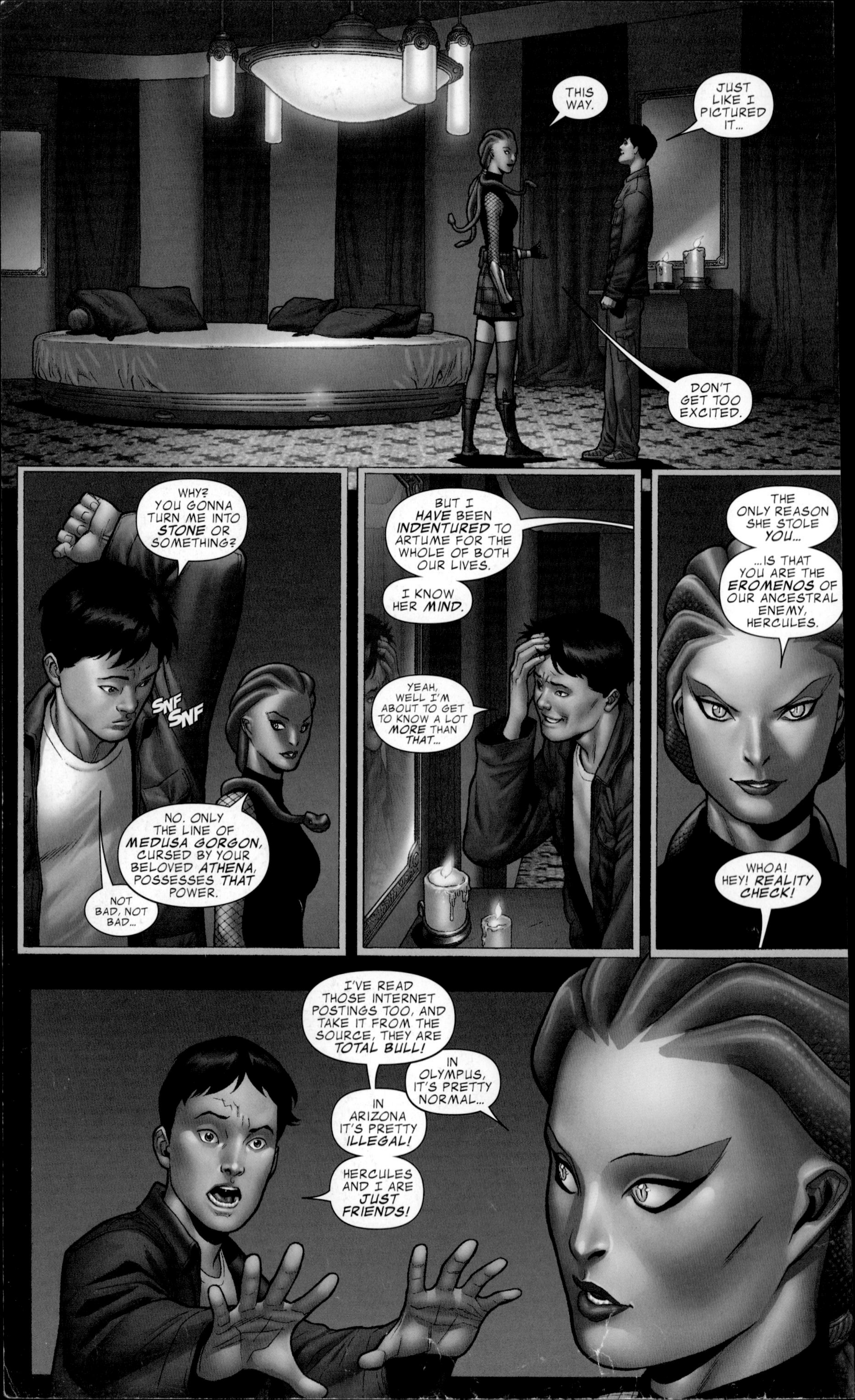
THIS WAY.
JUST LIKE I PICTURED IT...
DON'T GET TOO EXCITED.
WHY? YOU GONNA TURN ME INTO STONE OR SOMETHING?
SNF SNF
NO. ONLY THE LINE OF MEDUSA GORGON, CURSED BY YOUR BELOVED ATHENA, POSSESSES THAT POWER.
NOT BAD, NOT BAD...
BUT I HAVE BEEN INDENTURED TO ARTUME FOR THE WHOLE OF BOTH OUR LIVES.
I KNOW HER MIND.
YEAH, WELL I'M ABOUT TO GET TO KNOW A LOT MORE THAN THAT...
THE ONLY REASON SHE STOLE YOU...
...IS THAT YOU ARE THE EROMENOS OF OUR ANCESTRAL ENEMY, HERCULES.
WHOA! HEY! REALITY CHECK!
I'VE READ THOSE INTERNET POSTINGS TOO, AND TAKE IT FROM THE SOURCE, THEY ARE TOTAL BULL!
IN OLYMPUS, IT'S PRETTY NORMAL...
IN ARIZONA IT'S PRETTY ILLEGAL!
HERCULES AND I ARE JUST FRIENDS!

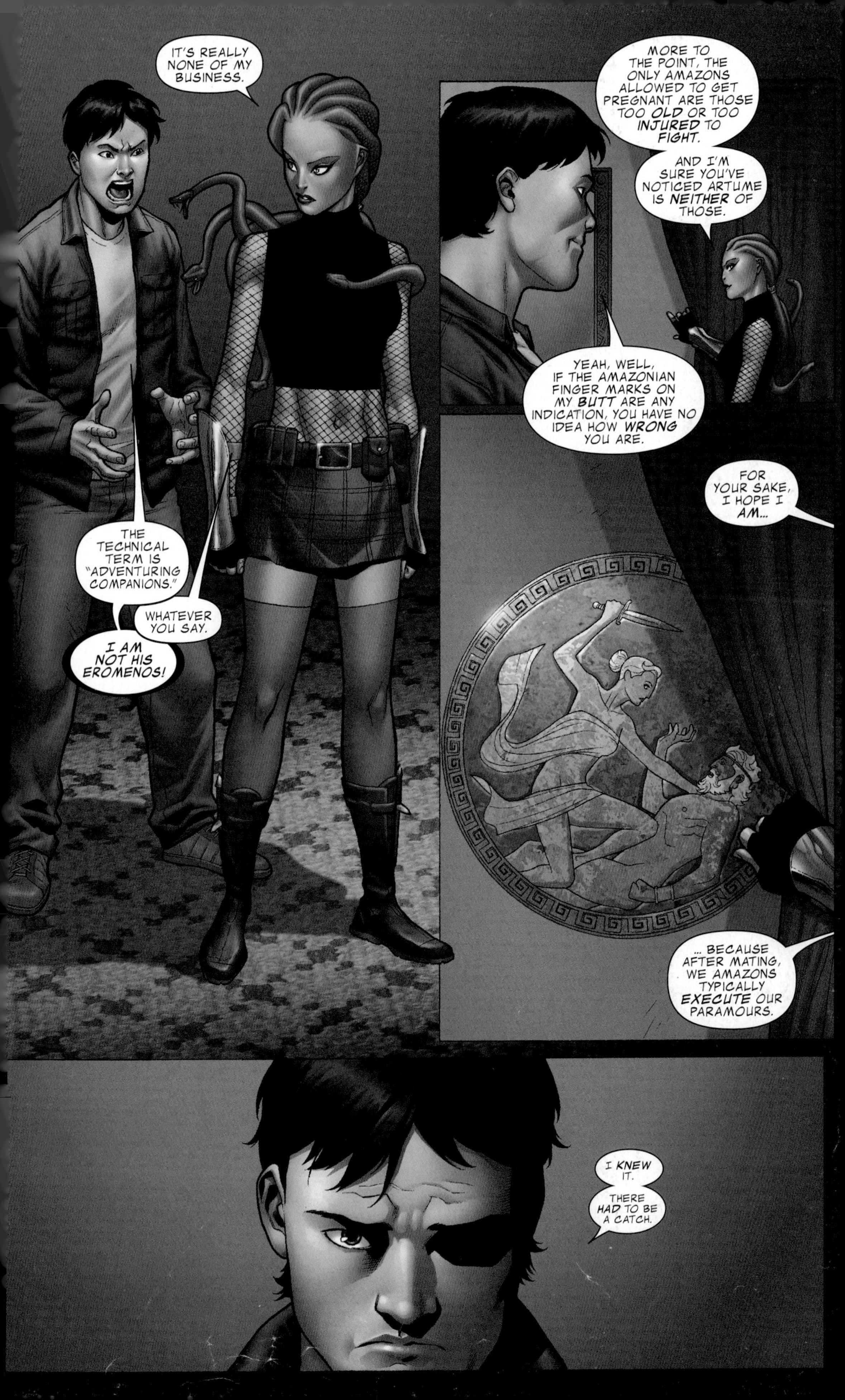
IT'S REALLY NONE OF MY BUSINESS.
THE TECHNICAL TERM IS "ADVENTURING COMPANIONS."
WHATEVER YOU SAY.
I AM NOT HIS EROMENOS!
MORE TO THE POINT, THE ONLY AMAZONS ALLOWED TO GET PREGNANT ARE THOSE TOO OLD OR TOO INJURED TO FIGHT.
AND I'M SURE YOU'VE NOTICED ARTUME IS NEITHER OF THOSE.
YEAH, WELL, IF THE AMAZONIAN FINGER MARKS ON MY BUTT ARE ANY INDICATION, YOU HAVE NO IDEA HOW WRONG YOU ARE.
FOR YOUR SAKE, I HOPE I AM...
... BECAUSE AFTER MATING, WE AMAZONS TYPICALLY EXECUTE OUR PARAMOURS.
I KNEW IT.
THERE HAD TO BE A CATCH.

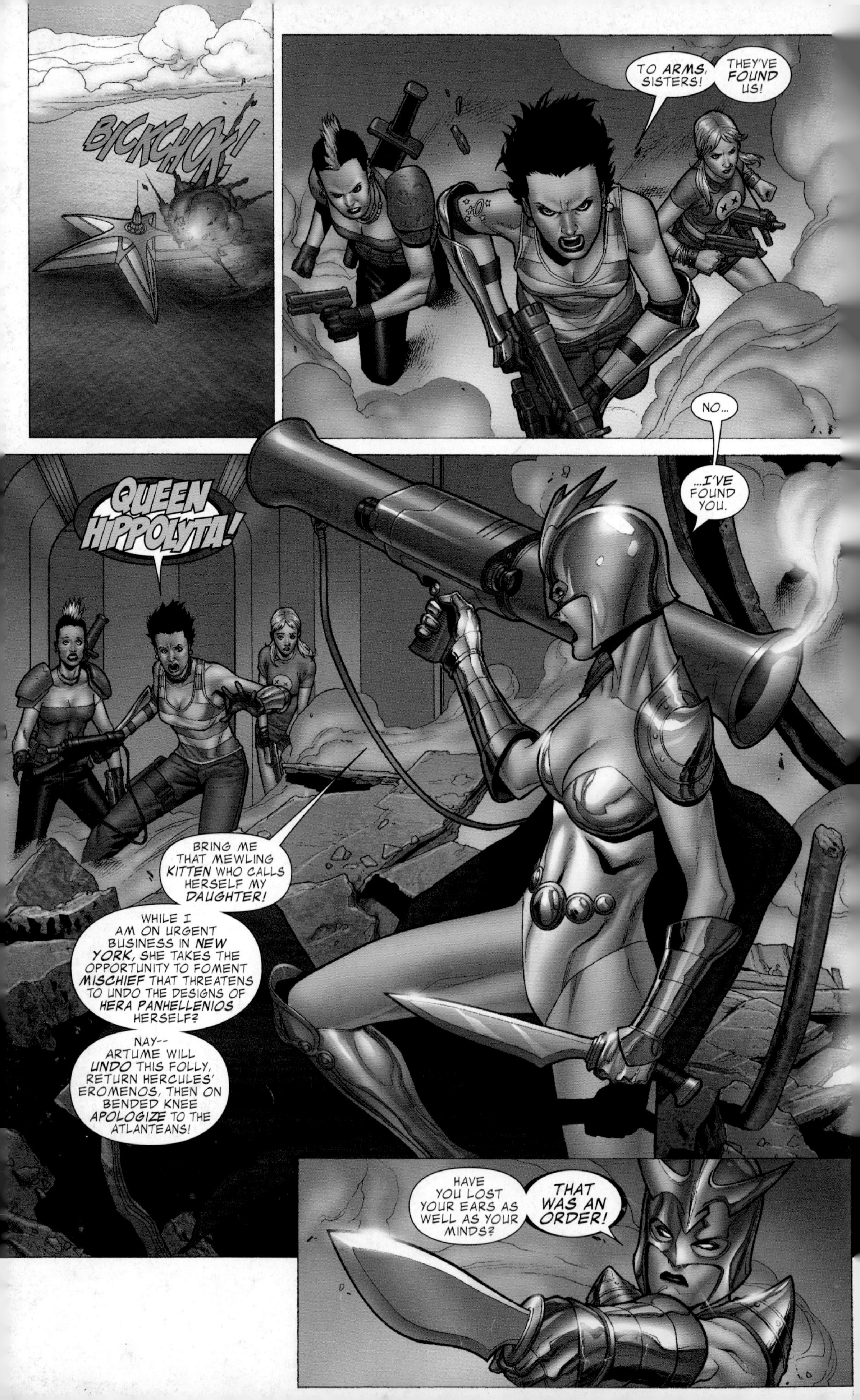
BICKCHOK!
TO ARMS, SISTERS!
THEY'VE FOUND US!
NO...
...I'VE FOUND YOU.
QUEEN HIPPOLYTA!
BRING ME THAT MEWLING KITTEN WHO CALLS HERSELF MY DAUGHTER!
WHILE I AM ON URGENT BUSINESS IN NEW YORK, SHE TAKES THE OPPORTUNITY TO FOMENT MISCHIEF THAT THREATENS TO UNDO THE DESIGNS OF HERA PANHELLENIOS HERSELF?
NAY-- ARTUME WILL UNDO THIS FOLLY, RETURN HERCULES' EROMENOS, THEN ON BENDED KNEE APOLOGIZE TO THE ATLANTEANS!
HAVE YOU LOST YOUR EARS AS WELL AS YOUR MINDS?
THAT WAS AN ORDER!

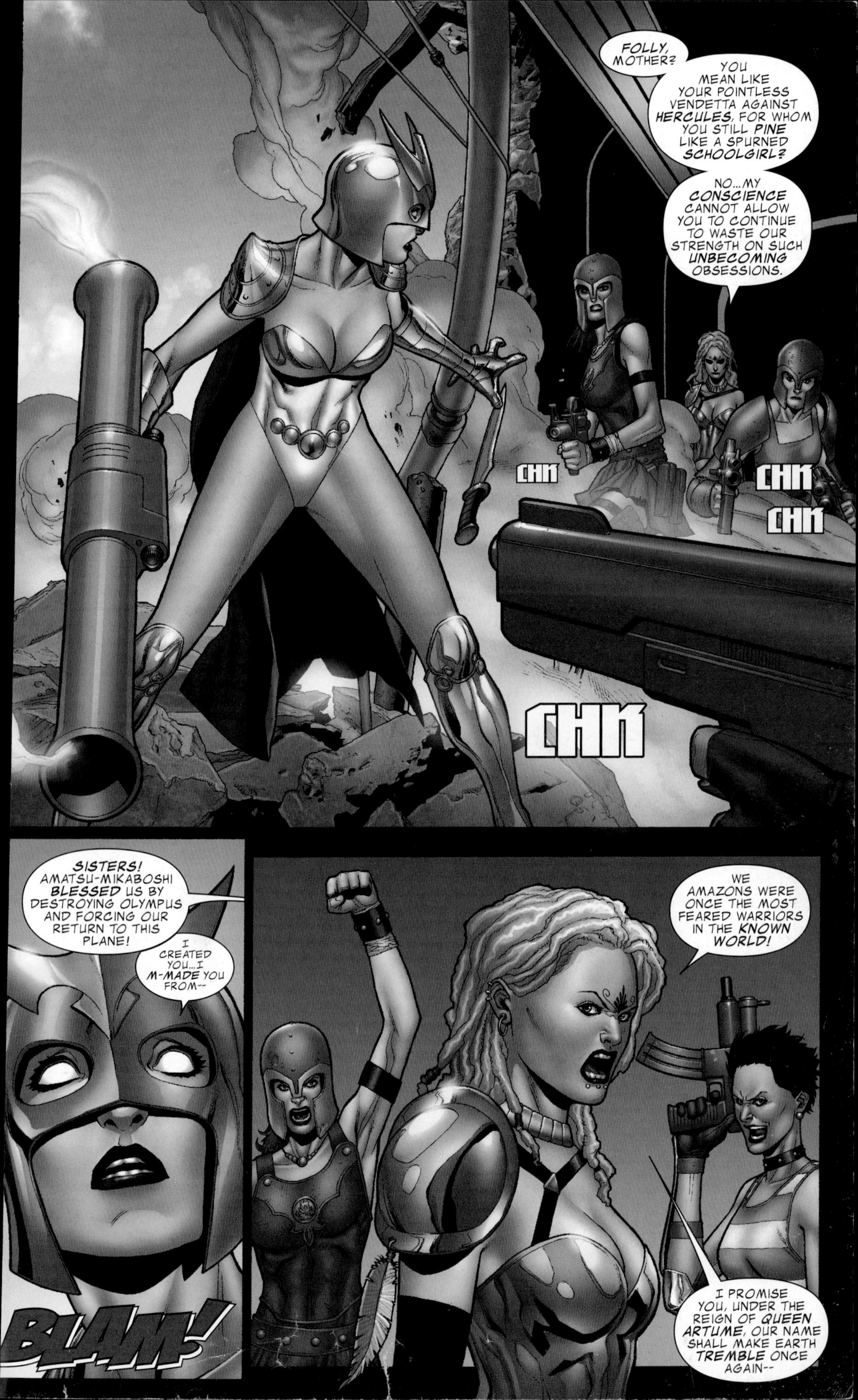

FOLLY, MOTHER?
YOU MEAN LIKE YOUR POINTLESS VENDETTA AGAINST HERCULES, FOR WHOM YOU STILL PINE LIKE A SPURNED SCHOOLGIRL?
NO...MY CONSCIENCE CANNOT ALLOW YOU TO CONTINUE TO WASTE OUR STRENGTH ON SUCH UNBECOMING OBSESSIONS.
CHK
CHK
CHK
CHK
SISTERS! AMATSU-MIKABOSHI BLESSED US BY DESTROYING OLYMPUS AND FORCING OUR RETURN TO THIS PLANE!
I CREATED YOU...I M-MADE YOU FROM--
WE AMAZONS WERE ONCE THE MOST FEARED WARRIORS IN THE KNOWN WORLD!
I PROMISE YOU, UNDER THE REIGN OF QUEEN ARTUME, OUR NAME SHALL MAKE EARTH TREMBLE ONCE AGAIN--
BLAM!

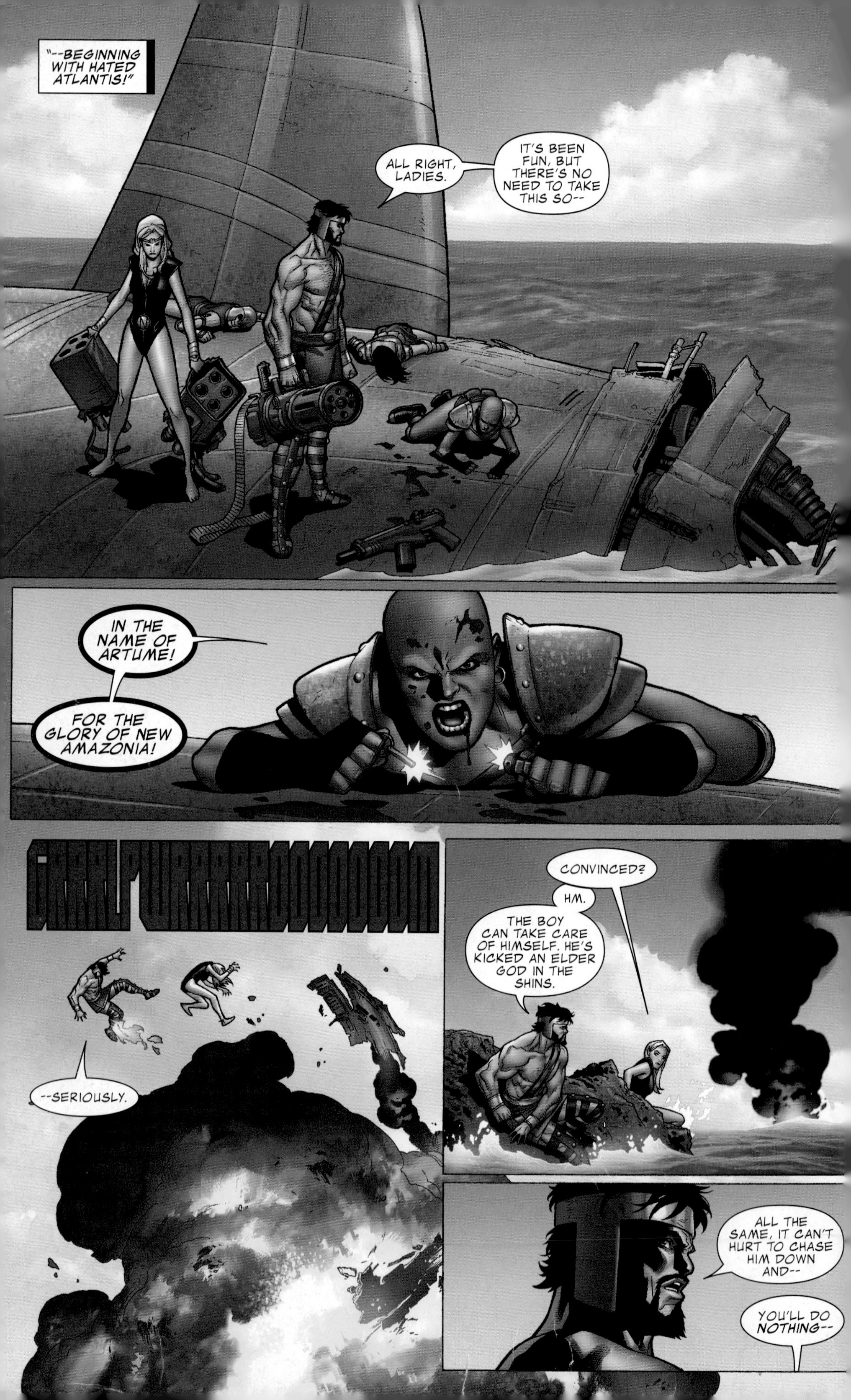
"--BEGINNING WITH HATED ATLANTIS!"
ALL RIGHT, LADIES.
IT'S BEEN FUN, BUT THERE'S NO NEED TO TAKE THIS SO--
IN THE NAME OF ARTUME!
FOR THE GLORY OF NEW AMAZONIA!
GRRRLPWRRRRROOOOOOOM
--SERIOUSLY.
CONVINCED?
HM.
THE BOY CAN TAKE CARE OF HIMSELF. HE'S KICKED AN ELDER GOD IN THE SHINS.
ALL THE SAME, IT CAN'T HURT TO CHASE HIM DOWN AND--
YOU'LL DO NOTHING--

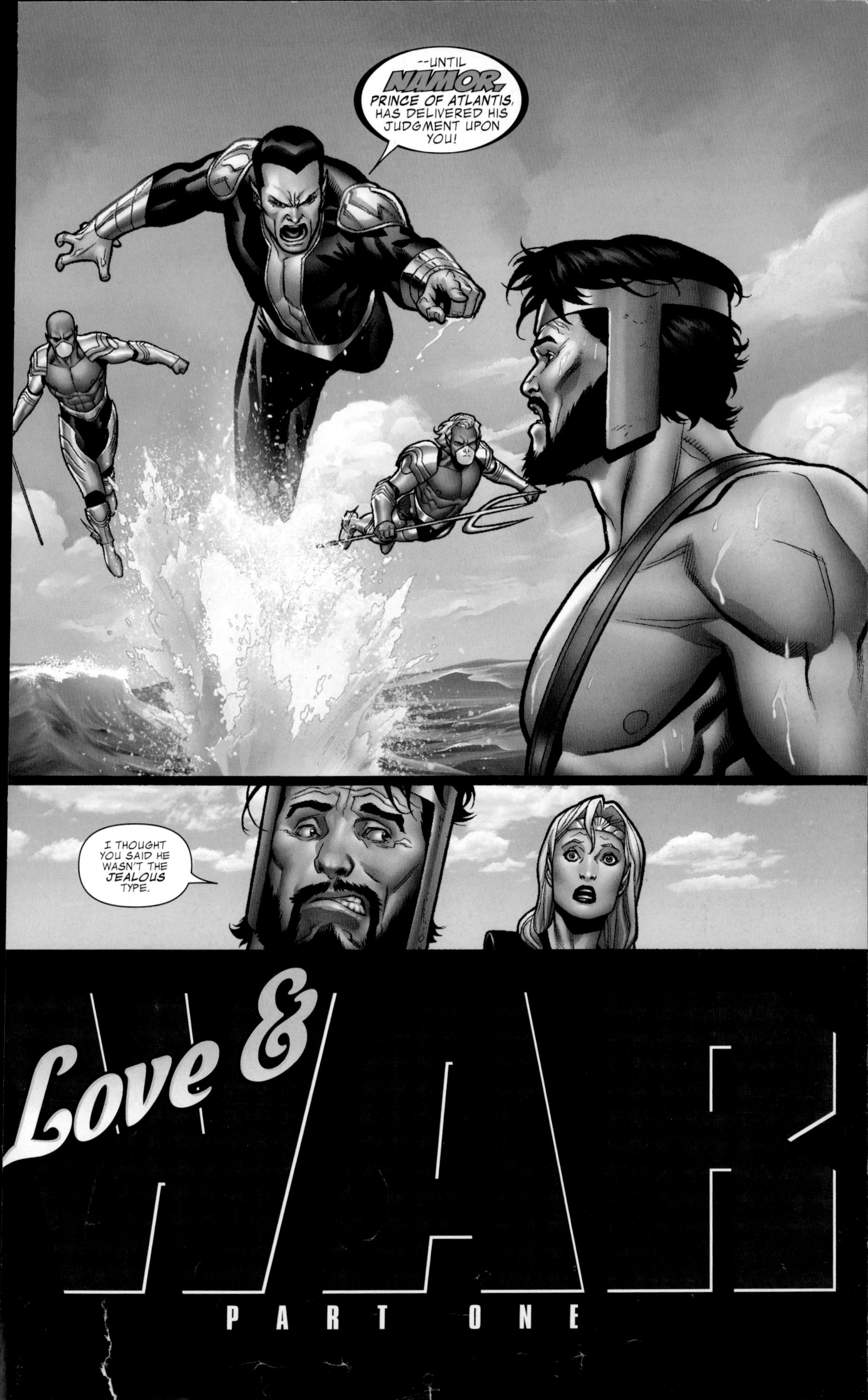
--UNTIL NAMOR, PRINCE OF ATLANTIS, HAS DELIVERED HIS JUDGMENT UPON YOU!
I THOUGHT YOU SAID HE WASN'T THE JEALOUS TYPE.
Love & WAR
PART ONE

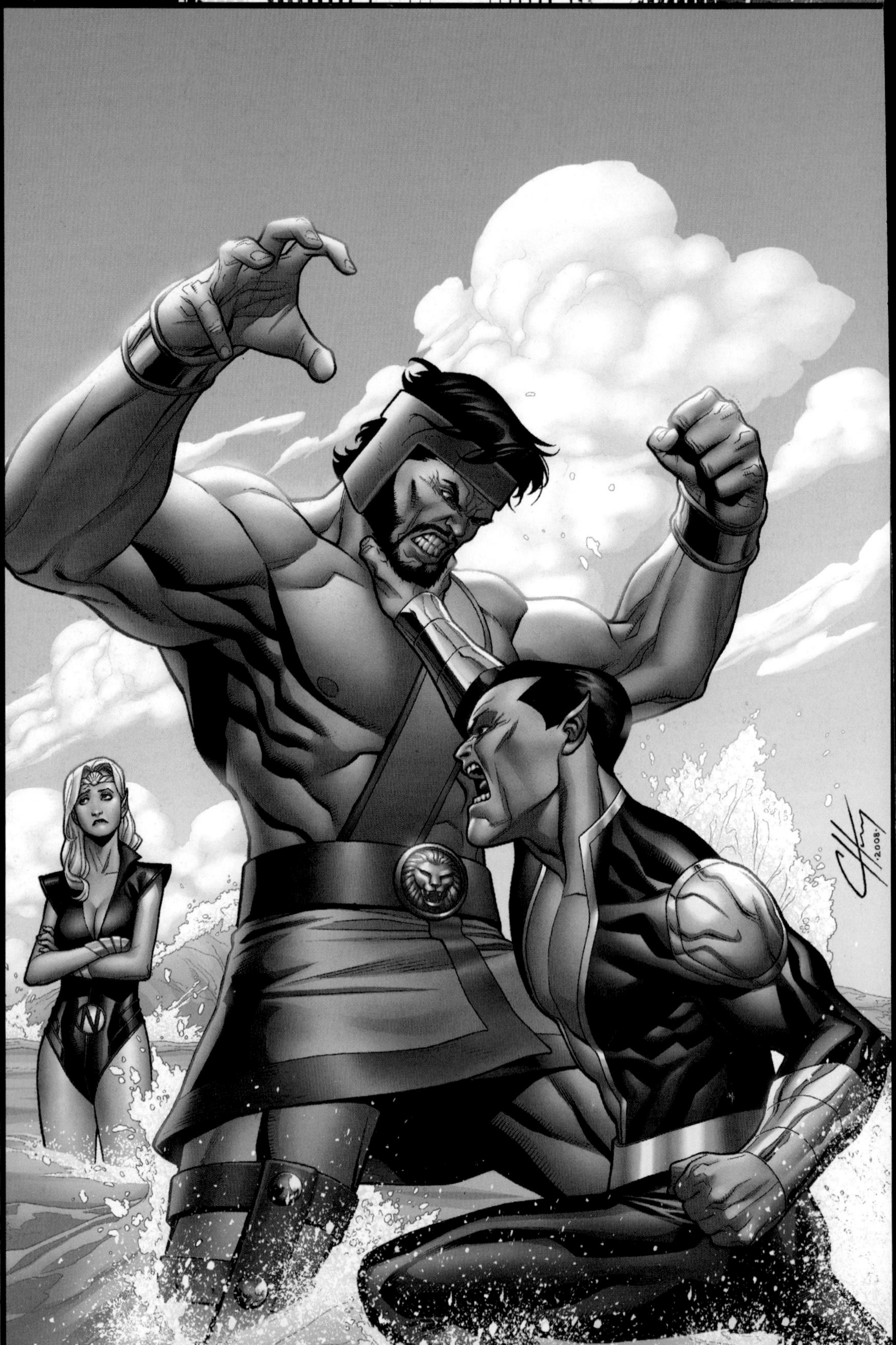

INCREDIBLE HERCULES #122

## SAPPHO 31 RELOADED

By Sappho of Lesbos, liberally edited by Amadeus Cho of Arizona

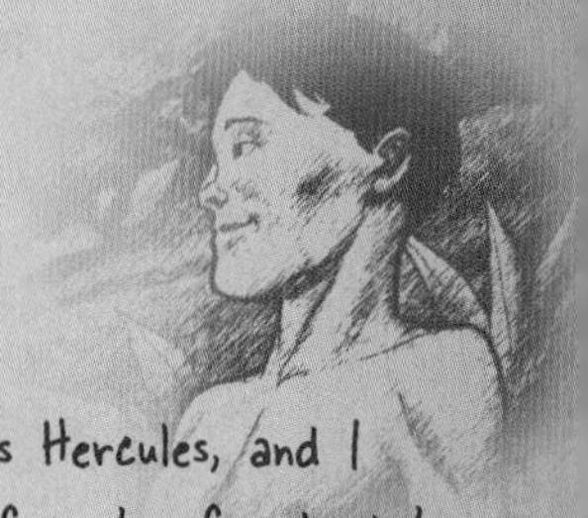

He seems to me, that man, ~~almost~~ is a god—
the man, who is face to face with you,
sitting close enough to you to hear
your sweet whispering

Yeah, his name's Hercules, and I Guarantee ya if you're female, he's just trying to get his swerve on

And your laughter, glistening, which
the heart in ~~my~~ Namora's (the SUB-MARINER'S cousin) breast beats for.
For when on you I glance, I do not,
not one sound, emit.

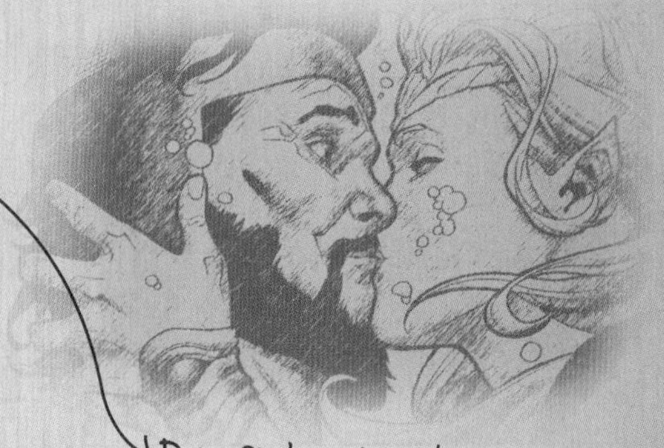

Duh, She's underwater.

But my tongue snaps, lightly
runs beneath my flesh a flame,
and from my eyes no light, and ~~rumbling~~ gunfire
comes into my ears,

cuz I've been captured by armed Amazons that want to use my body for breeding and... pleasure

And my skin grows damp, and trembling
all over racks me, and greener than the ~~grass~~ seaweed
am I, and one step short of dying
~~I seem to myself.~~

is Here, cuz SUB-MARINER just showed up to sub-marinate his @!!$$!!. . .

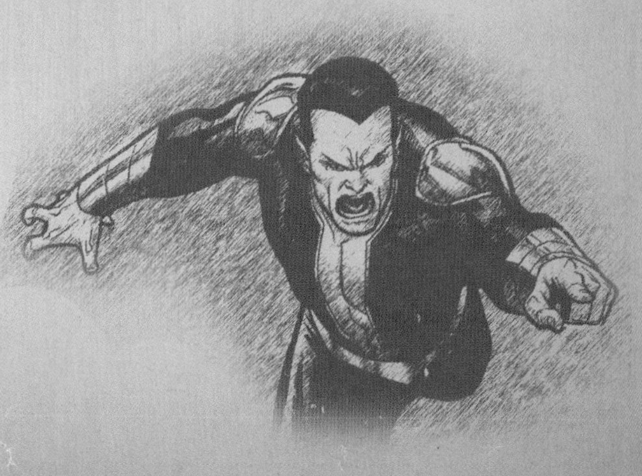

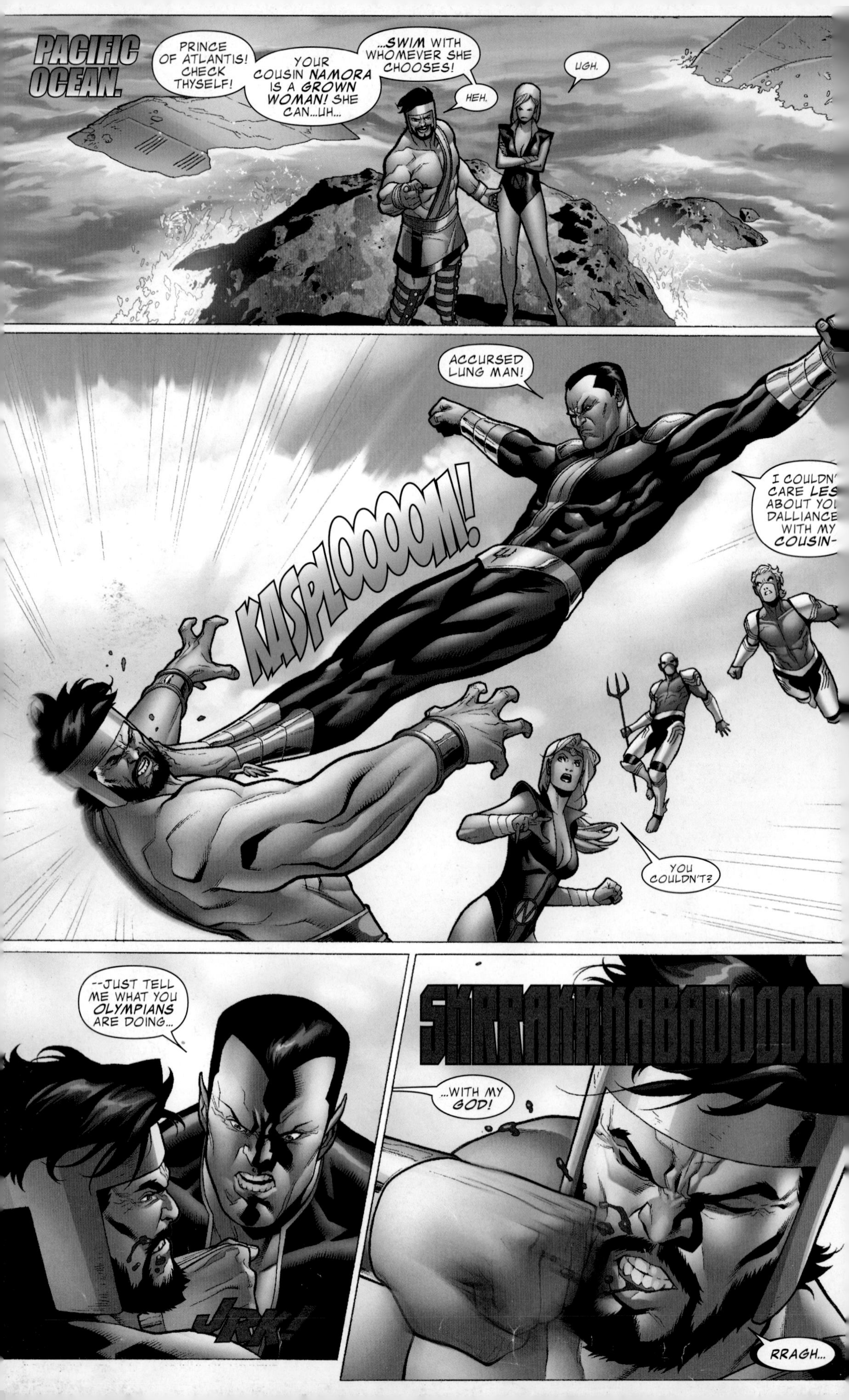
PACIFIC OCEAN.
PRINCE OF ATLANTIS! CHECK THYSELF!
YOUR COUSIN NAMORA IS A GROWN WOMAN! SHE CAN...UH...
...SWIM WITH WHOMEVER SHE CHOOSES!
HEH.
UGH.
ACCURSED LUNG MAN!
KASPLOOOOM!
I COULDN' CARE LES ABOUT YO DALLIANCE WITH MY COUSIN-
YOU COULDN'T?
--JUST TELL ME WHAT YOU OLYMPIANS ARE DOING...
JKK!
SKRAKKKABADOOOM
...WITH MY GOD!
RRAGH...

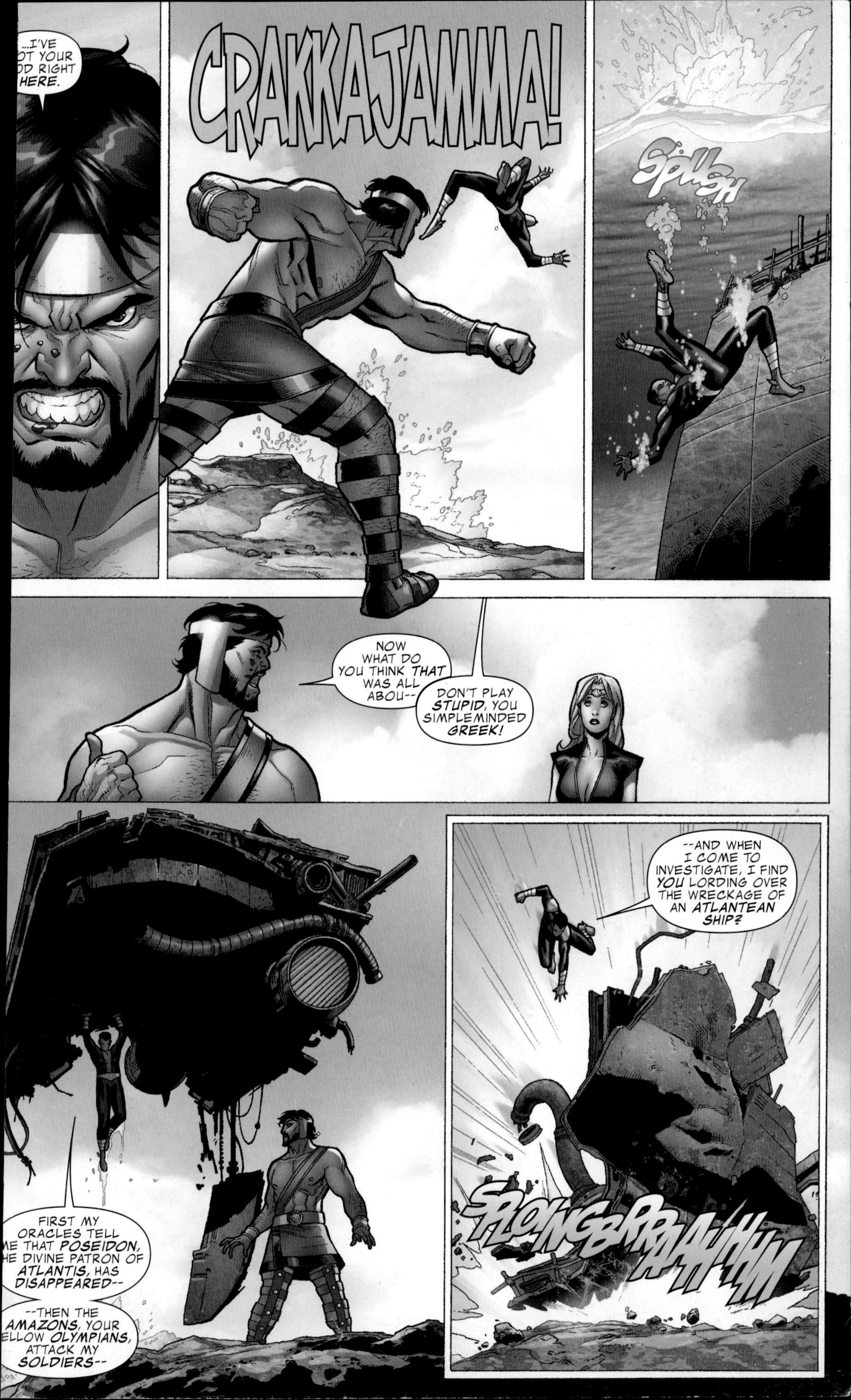

...I'VE
OT YOUR
OD RIGHT
HERE.
CRAKKAJAMMA!
SPLUSH
NOW WHAT DO YOU THINK THAT WAS ALL ABOU--
DON'T PLAY STUPID, YOU SIMPLEMINDED GREEK!
FIRST MY ORACLES TELL
ME THAT POSEIDON,
HE DIVINE PATRON OF ATLANTIS, HAS DISAPPEARED--
--THEN THE AMAZONS, YOUR
ELLOW OLYMPIANS, ATTACK MY SOLDIERS--
--AND WHEN I COME TO INVESTIGATE, I FIND YOU LORDING OVER THE WRECKAGE OF AN ATLANTEAN SHIP?
SPLONGBRRAAHHM

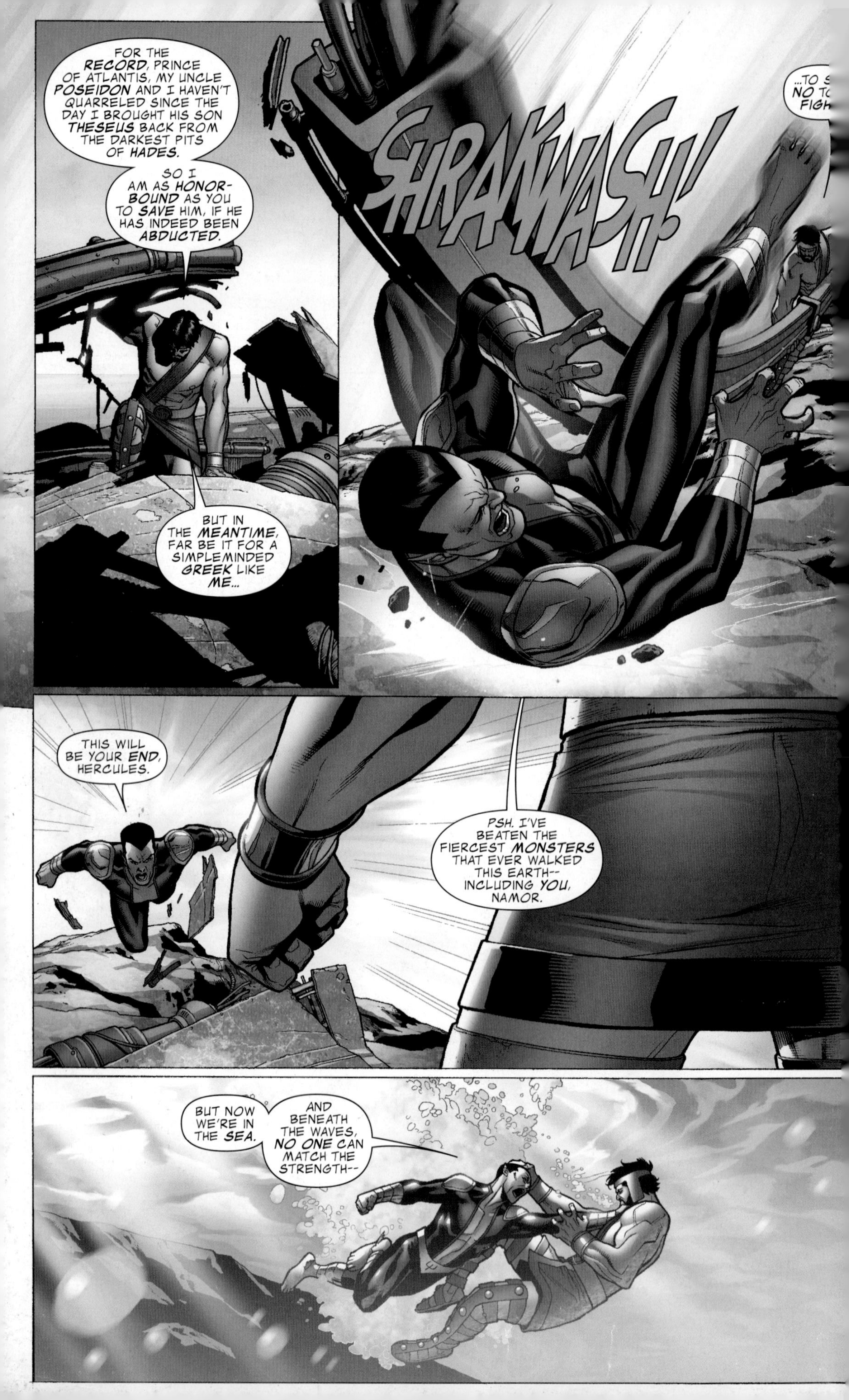
FOR THE RECORD, PRINCE OF ATLANTIS, MY UNCLE POSEIDON AND I HAVEN'T QUARRELED SINCE THE DAY I BROUGHT HIS SON THESEUS BACK FROM THE DARKEST PITS OF HADES.
SO I AM AS HONOR-BOUND AS YOU TO SAVE HIM, IF HE HAS INDEED BEEN ABDUCTED.
BUT IN THE MEANTIME, FAR BE IT FOR A SIMPLEMINDED GREEK LIKE ME...
SHRAKWASH!
THIS WILL BE YOUR END, HERCULES.
PSH. I'VE BEATEN THE FIERCEST MONSTERS THAT EVER WALKED THIS EARTH-- INCLUDING YOU, NAMOR.
BUT NOW WE'RE IN THE SEA.
AND BENEATH THE WAVES, NO ONE CAN MATCH THE STRENGTH--

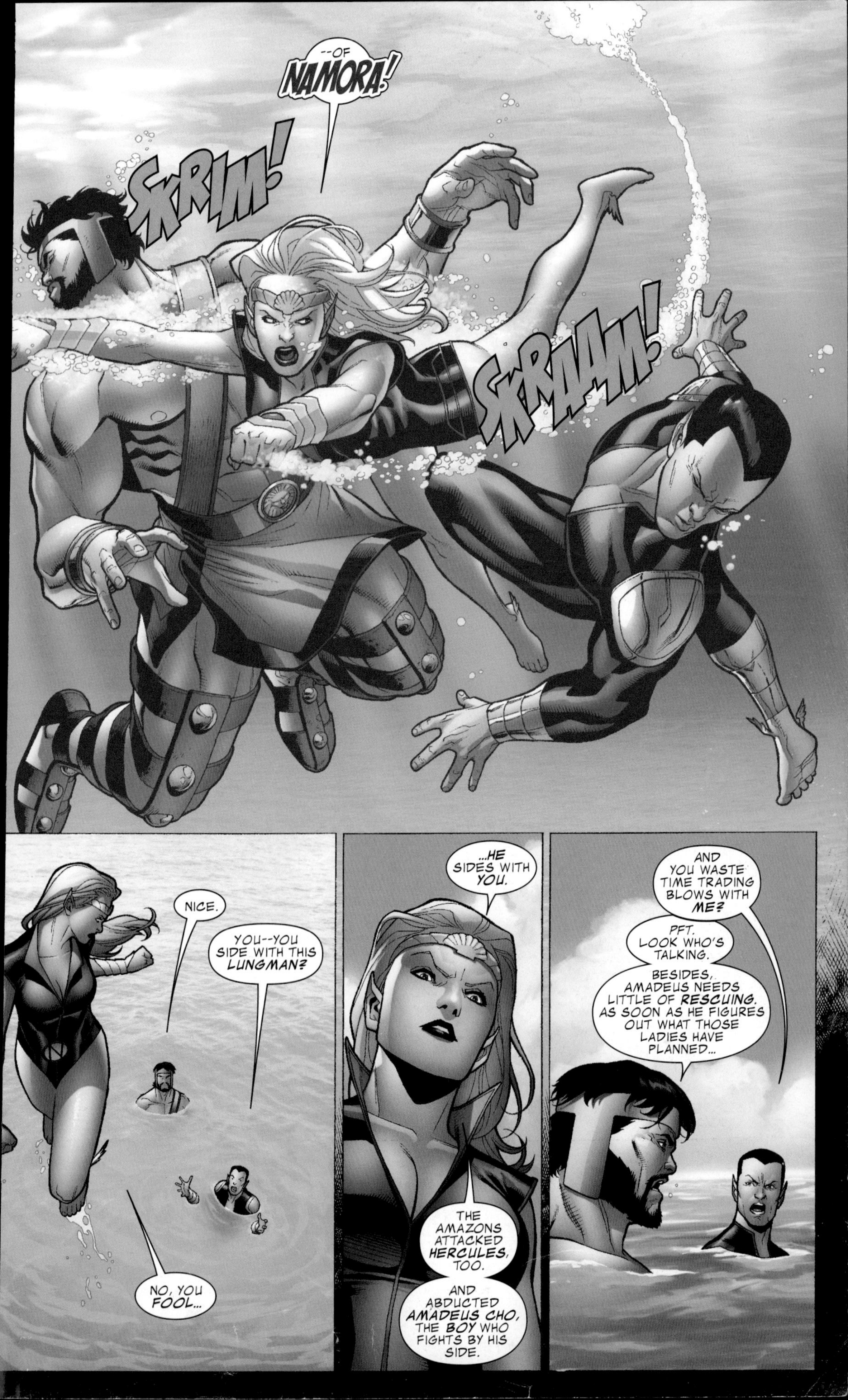
--OF NAMORA!
SKRIM!
SKRAAM!
NICE.
YOU--YOU SIDE WITH THIS LUNGMAN?
NO, YOU FOOL...
...HE SIDES WITH YOU.
THE AMAZONS ATTACKED HERCULES, TOO.
AND ABDUCTED AMADEUS CHO, THE BOY WHO FIGHTS BY HIS SIDE.
AND YOU WASTE TIME TRADING BLOWS WITH ME?
PFT. LOOK WHO'S TALKING.
BESIDES, AMADEUS NEEDS LITTLE OF RESCUING. AS SOON AS HE FIGURES OUT WHAT THOSE LADIES HAVE PLANNED...

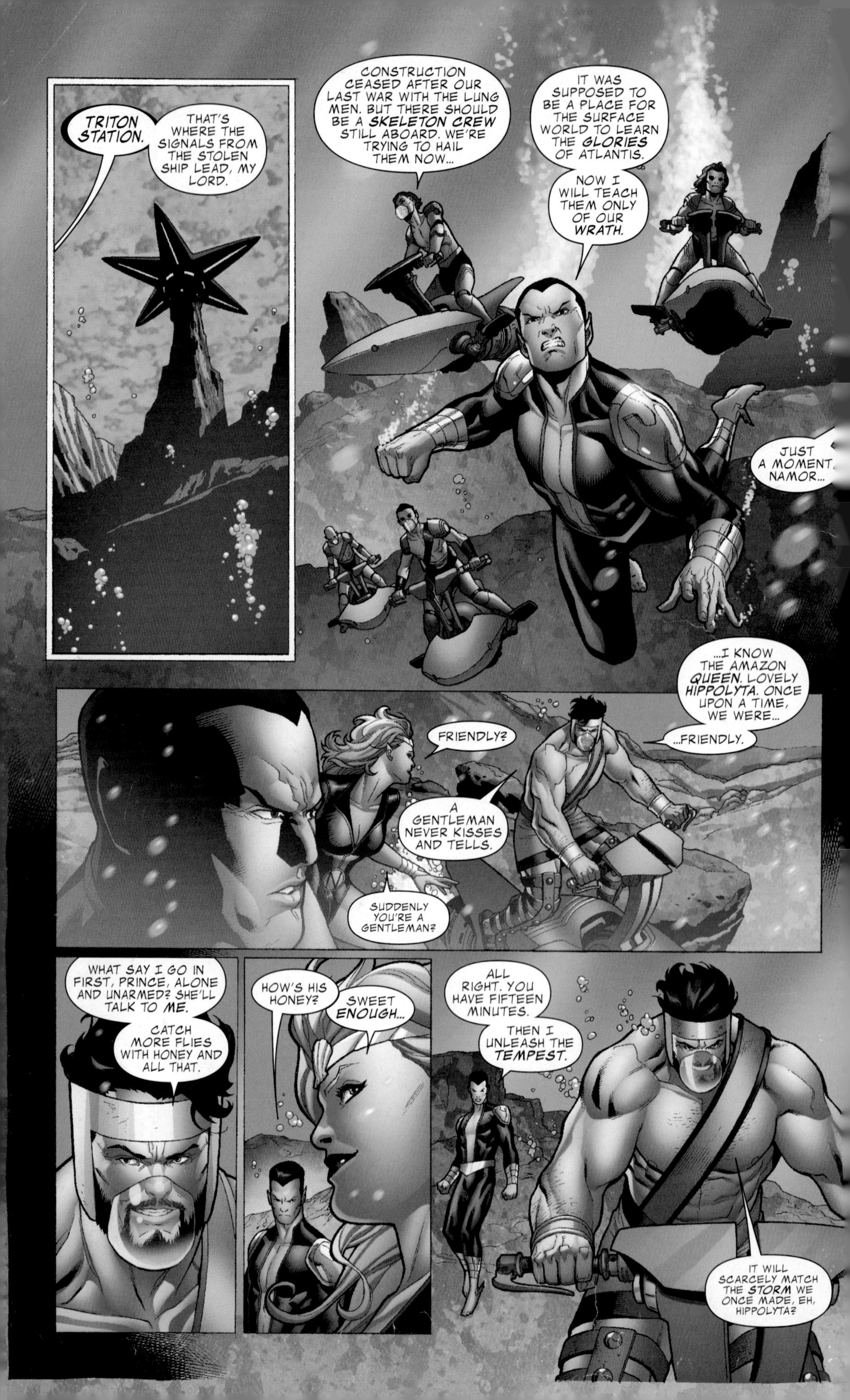

TRITON STATION.
THAT'S WHERE THE SIGNALS FROM THE STOLEN SHIP LEAD, MY LORD.
CONSTRUCTION CEASED AFTER OUR LAST WAR WITH THE LUNG MEN. BUT THERE SHOULD BE A SKELETON CREW STILL ABOARD. WE'RE TRYING TO HAIL THEM NOW...
IT WAS SUPPOSED TO BE A PLACE FOR THE SURFACE WORLD TO LEARN THE GLORIES OF ATLANTIS.
NOW I WILL TEACH THEM ONLY OF OUR WRATH.
JUST A MOMENT, NAMOR...
...I KNOW THE AMAZON QUEEN. LOVELY HIPPOLYTA. ONCE UPON A TIME, WE WERE...
...FRIENDLY.
FRIENDLY?
A GENTLEMAN NEVER KISSES AND TELLS.
SUDDENLY YOU'RE A GENTLEMAN?
WHAT SAY I GO IN FIRST, PRINCE, ALONE AND UNARMED? SHE'LL TALK TO ME.
CATCH MORE FLIES WITH HONEY AND ALL THAT.
HOW'S HIS HONEY?
SWEET ENOUGH...
ALL RIGHT. YOU HAVE FIFTEEN MINUTES.
THEN I UNLEASH THE TEMPEST.
IT WILL SCARCELY MATCH THE STORM WE ONCE MADE, EH, HIPPOLYTA?

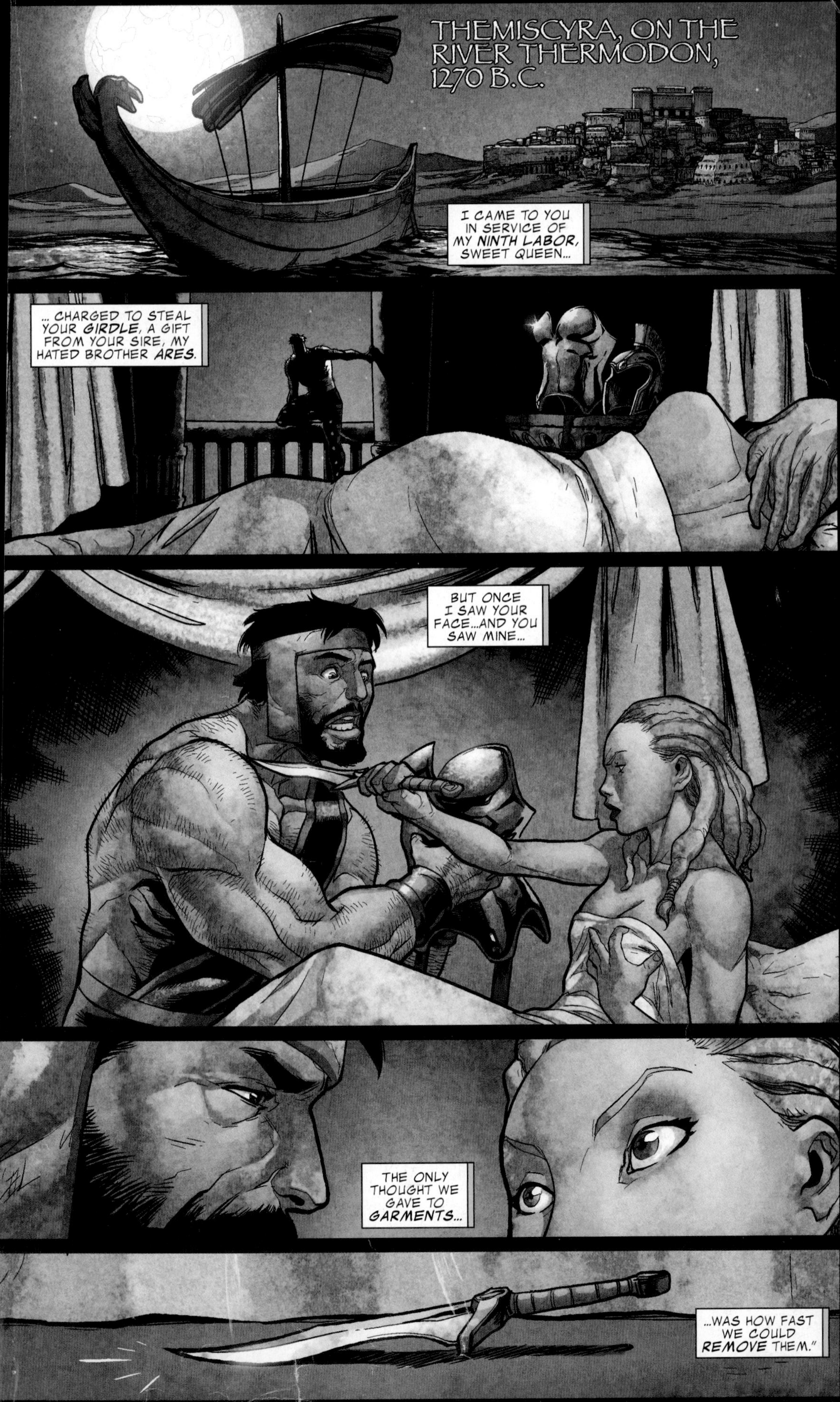
THEMISCYRA, ON THE RIVER THERMODON, 1270 B.C.
I CAME TO YOU IN SERVICE OF MY NINTH LABOR, SWEET QUEEN...
... CHARGED TO STEAL YOUR GIRDLE, A GIFT FROM YOUR SIRE, MY HATED BROTHER ARES.
BUT ONCE I SAW YOUR FACE...AND YOU SAW MINE...
THE ONLY THOUGHT WE GAVE TO GARMENTS...
...WAS HOW FAST WE COULD REMOVE THEM."

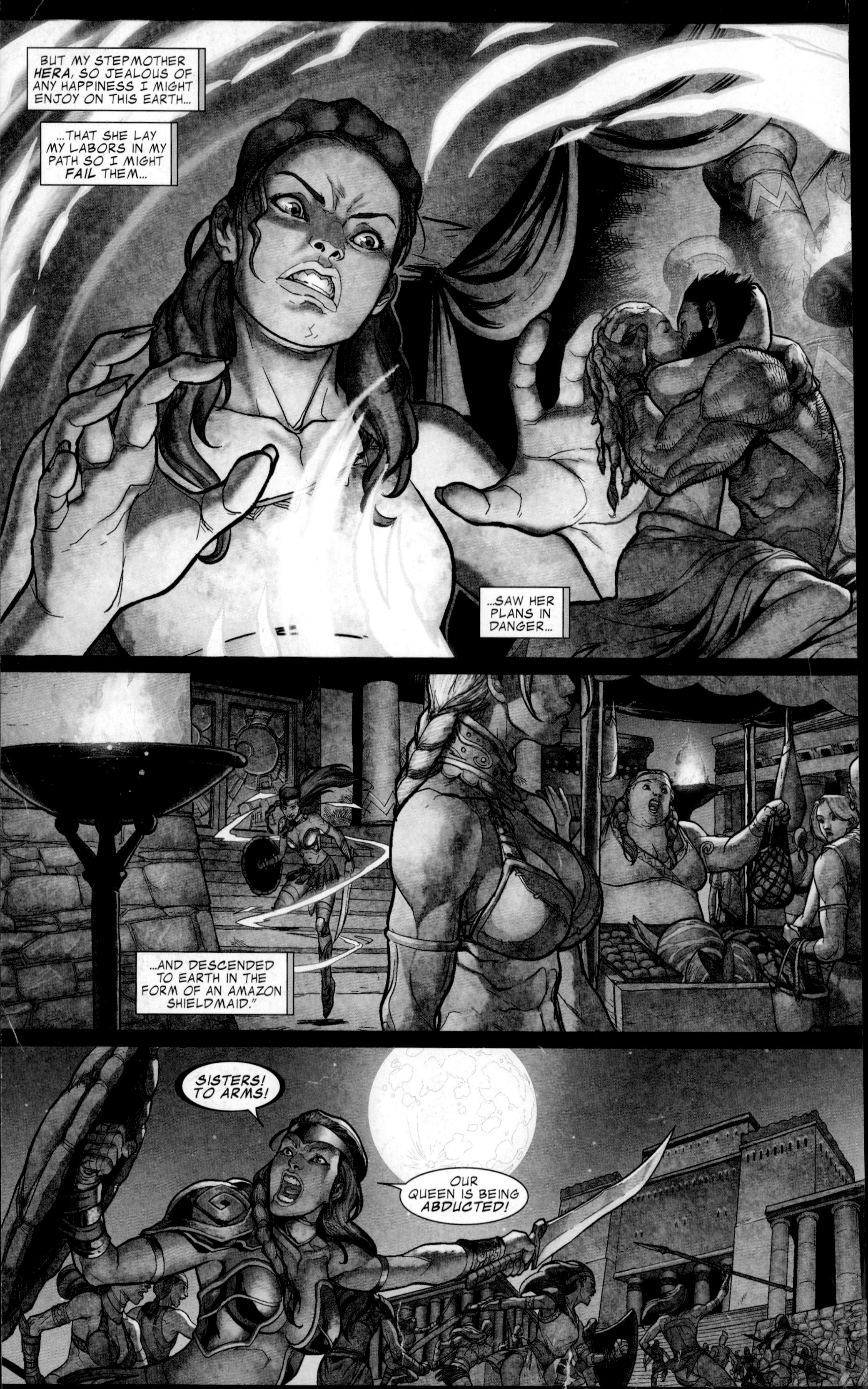
BUT MY STEPMOTHER HERA, SO JEALOUS OF ANY HAPPINESS I MIGHT ENJOY ON THIS EARTH...
...THAT SHE LAY MY LABORS IN MY PATH SO I MIGHT FAIL THEM...
...SAW HER PLANS IN DANGER...
...AND DESCENDED TO EARTH IN THE FORM OF AN AMAZON SHIELDMAID."
SISTERS! TO ARMS!
OUR QUEEN IS BEING ABDUCTED!

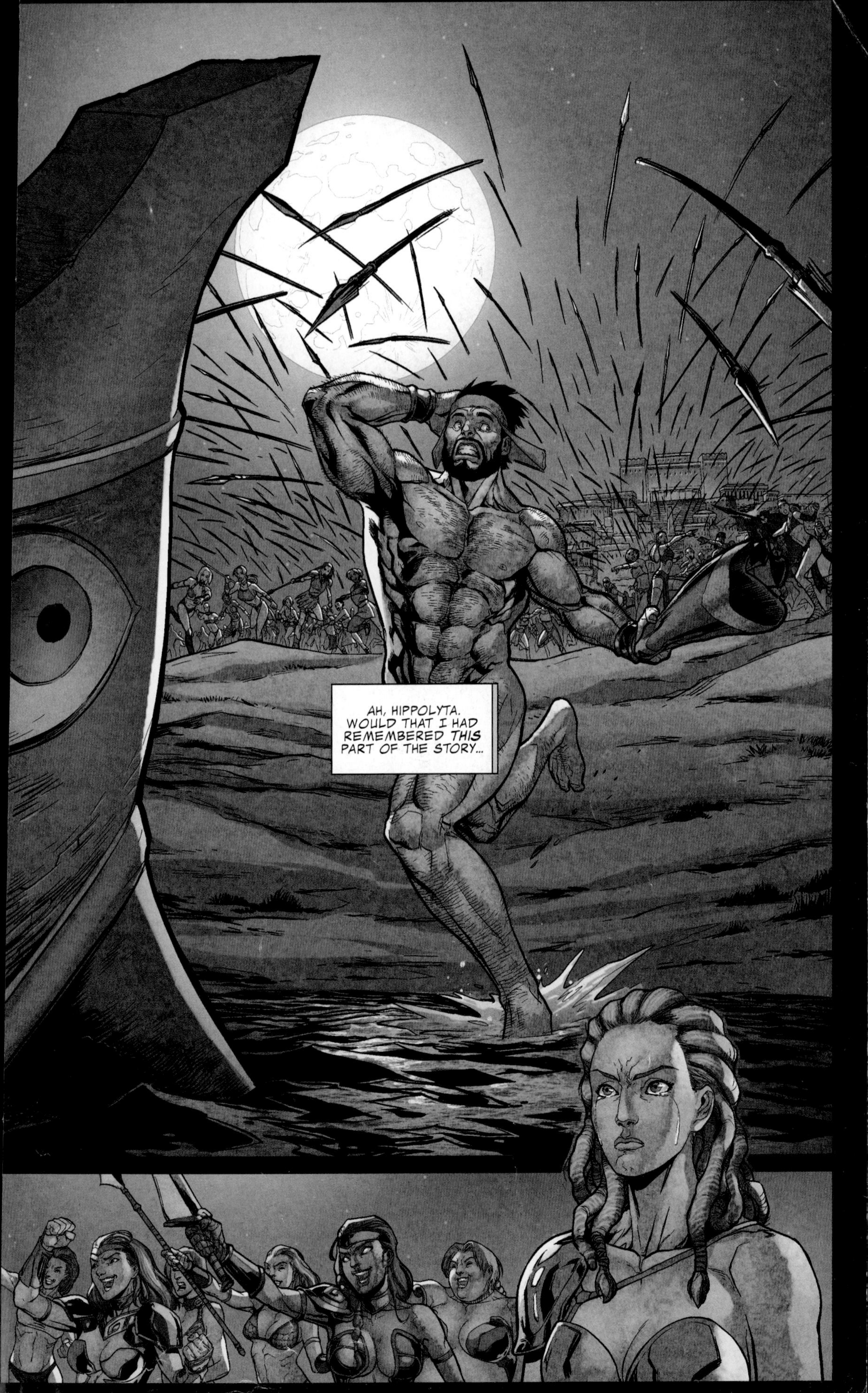
AH, HIPPOLYTA. WOULD THAT I HAD REMEMBERED THIS PART OF THE STORY...

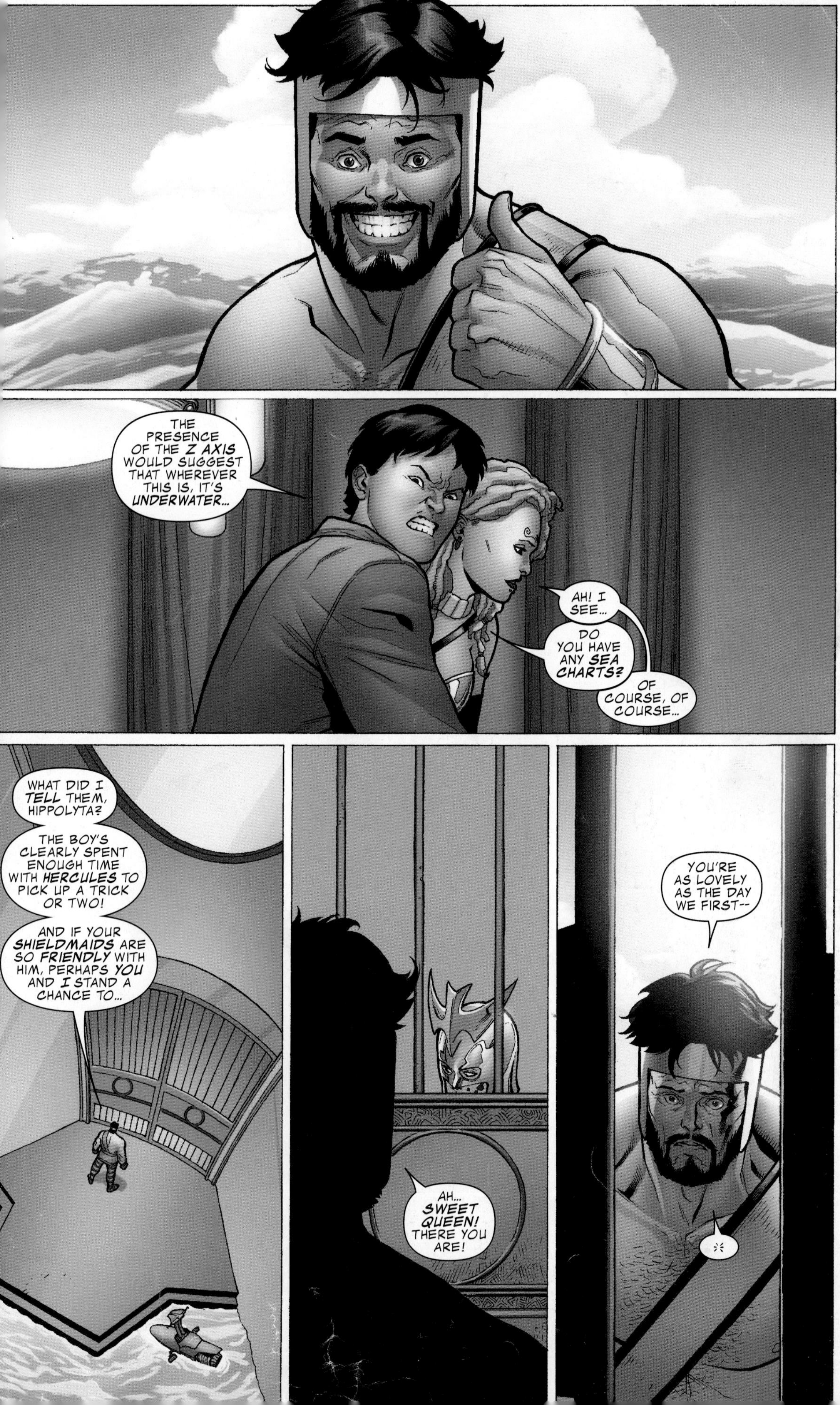
THE PRESENCE OF THE Z AXIS WOULD SUGGEST THAT WHEREVER THIS IS, IT'S UNDERWATER...
AH! I SEE...
DO YOU HAVE ANY SEA CHARTS?
OF COURSE, OF COURSE...
WHAT DID I TELL THEM, HIPPOLYTA?
THE BOY'S CLEARLY SPENT ENOUGH TIME WITH HERCULES TO PICK UP A TRICK OR TWO!
AND IF YOUR SHIELDMAIDS ARE SO FRIENDLY WITH HIM, PERHAPS YOU AND I STAND A CHANCE TO...
AH... SWEET QUEEN! THERE YOU ARE!
YOU'RE AS LOVELY AS THE DAY WE FIRST--

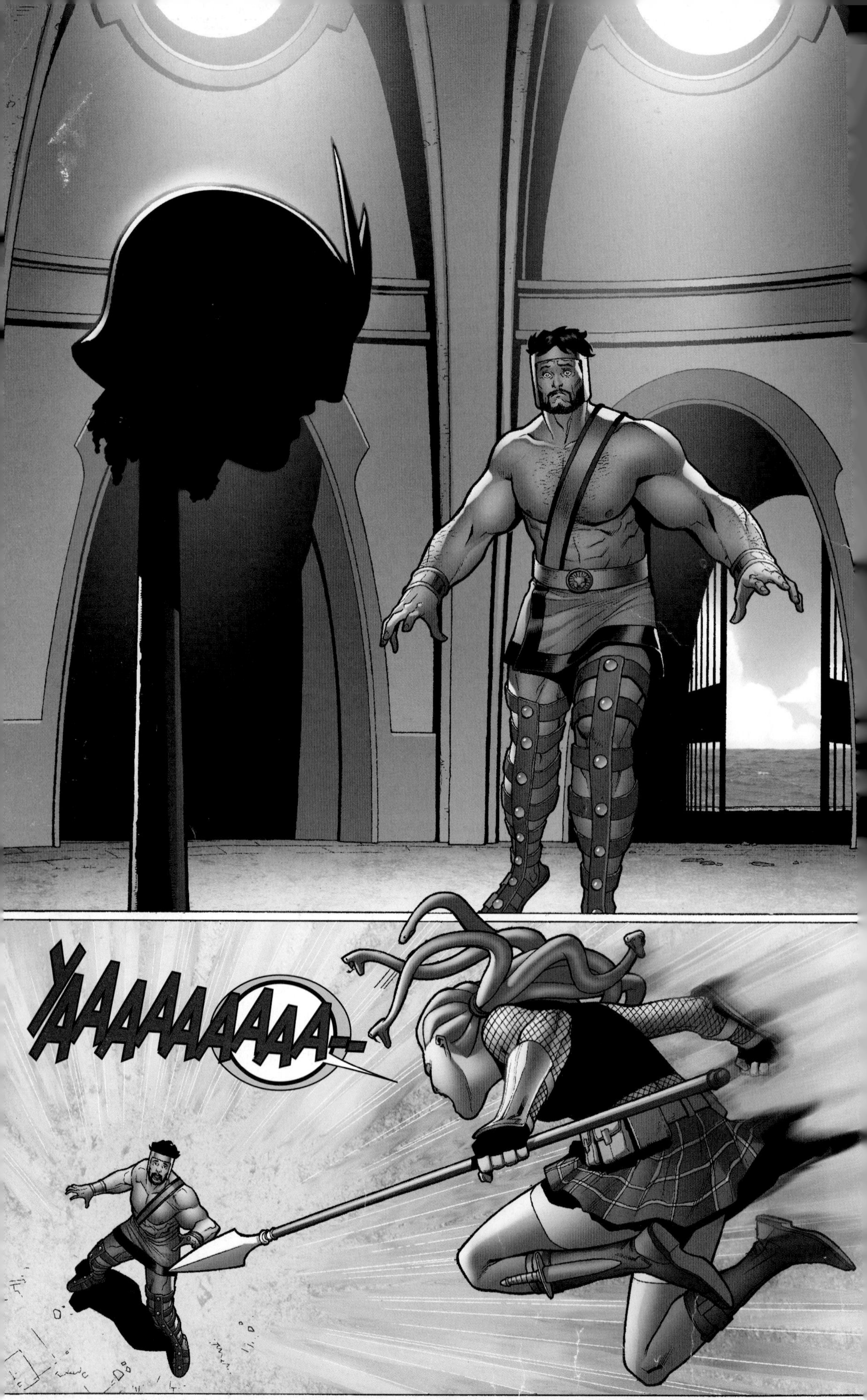
YAAAAAAAAA--

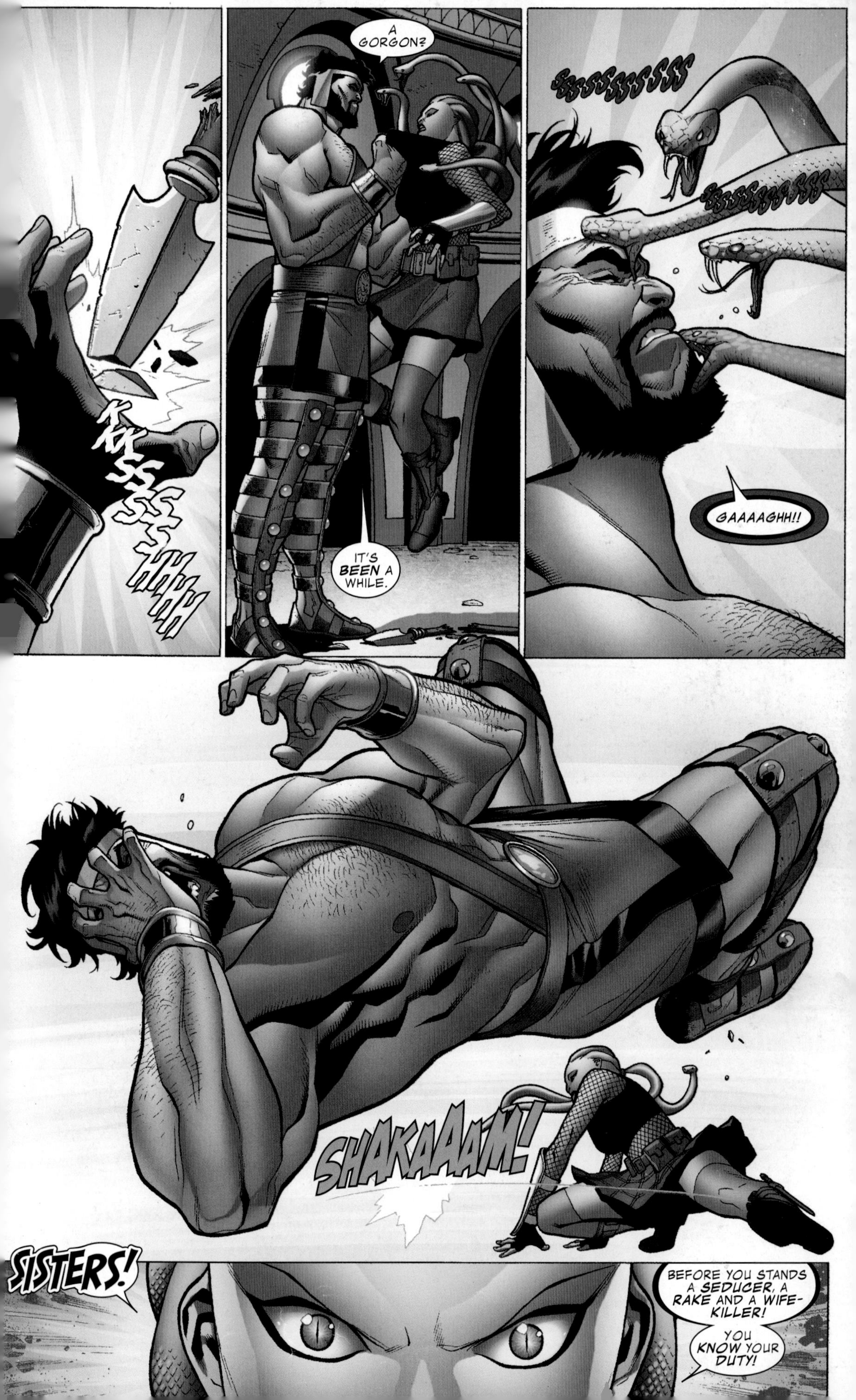

KKSSSSHHHH
A GORGON?
IT'S BEEN A WHILE.
SSSSSSSSSSSS
SSSSSSSSSSSS
GAAAAGHH!!
SHAKAAAM!
SISTERS!
BEFORE YOU STANDS A SEDUCER, A RAKE AND A WIFE-KILLER!
YOU KNOW YOUR DUTY!

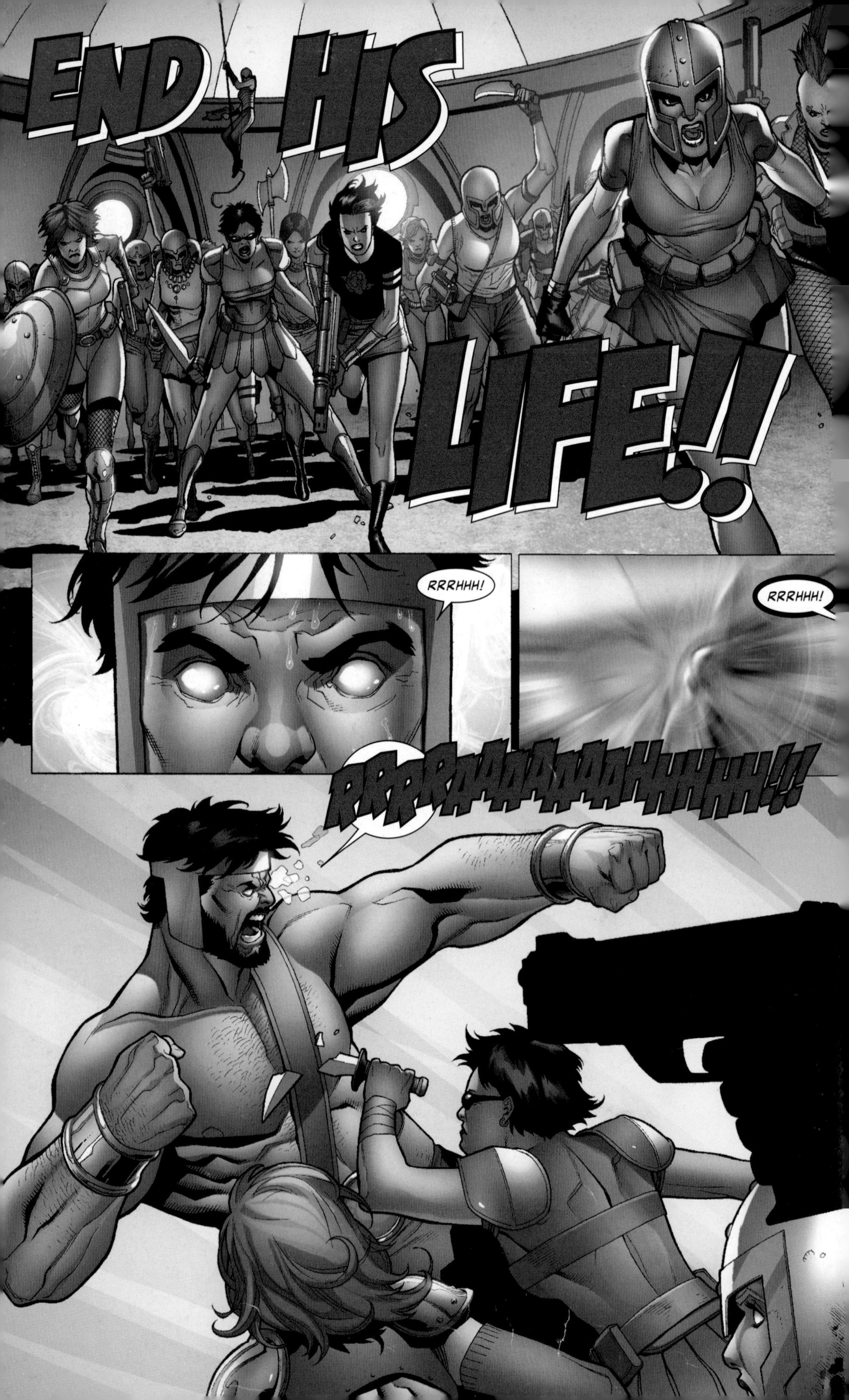
END HIS LIFE!!
RRRHHH!
RRRHHH!
RRRRAAAAAAAHHHHH!!!

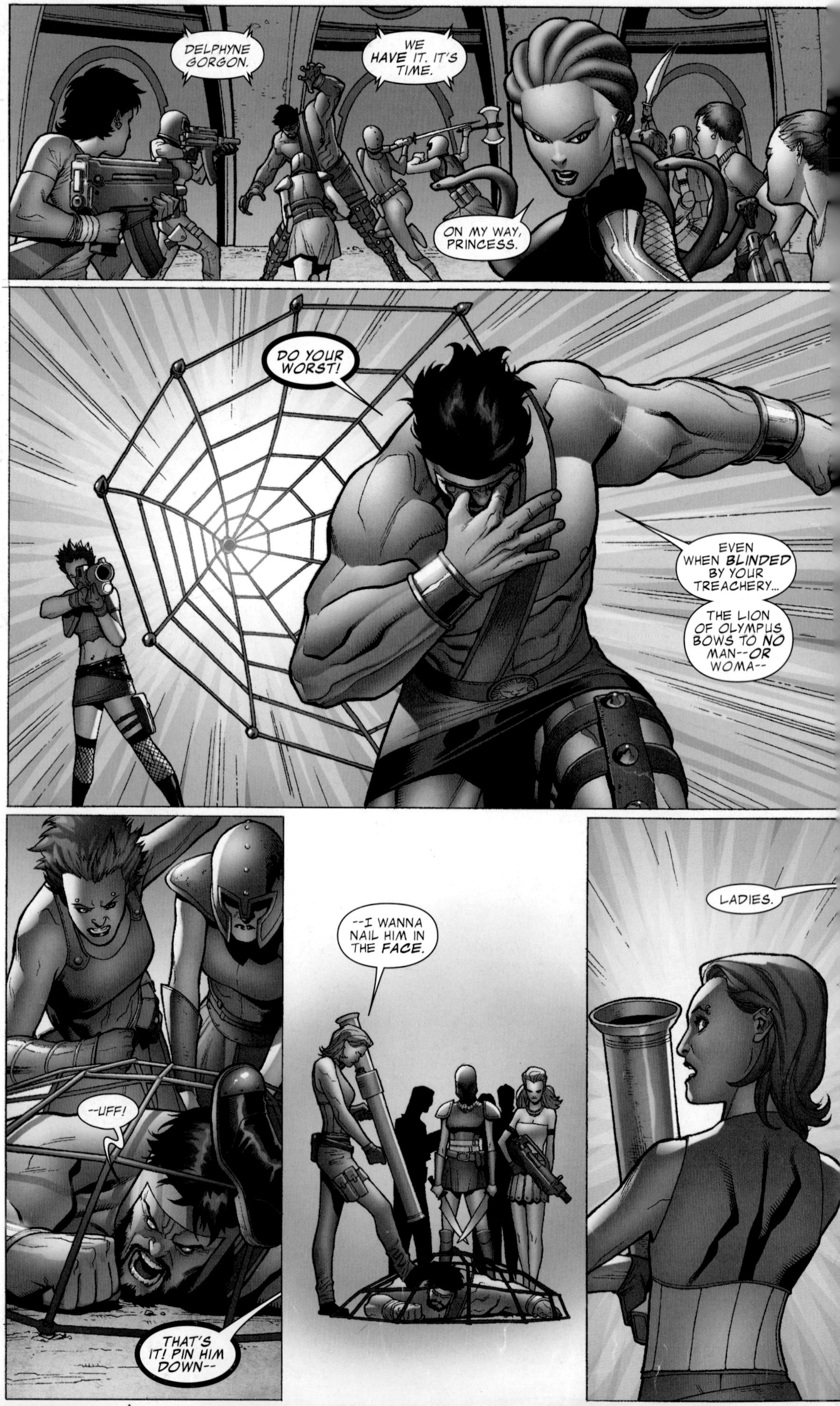
DELPHYNE GORGON.
WE HAVE IT. IT'S TIME.
ON MY WAY, PRINCESS.
DO YOUR WORST!
EVEN WHEN BLINDED BY YOUR TREACHERY...
THE LION OF OLYMPUS BOWS TO NO MAN--OR WOMA--
--UFF!
THAT'S IT! PIN HIM DOWN--
--I WANNA NAIL HIM IN THE FACE.
LADIES.

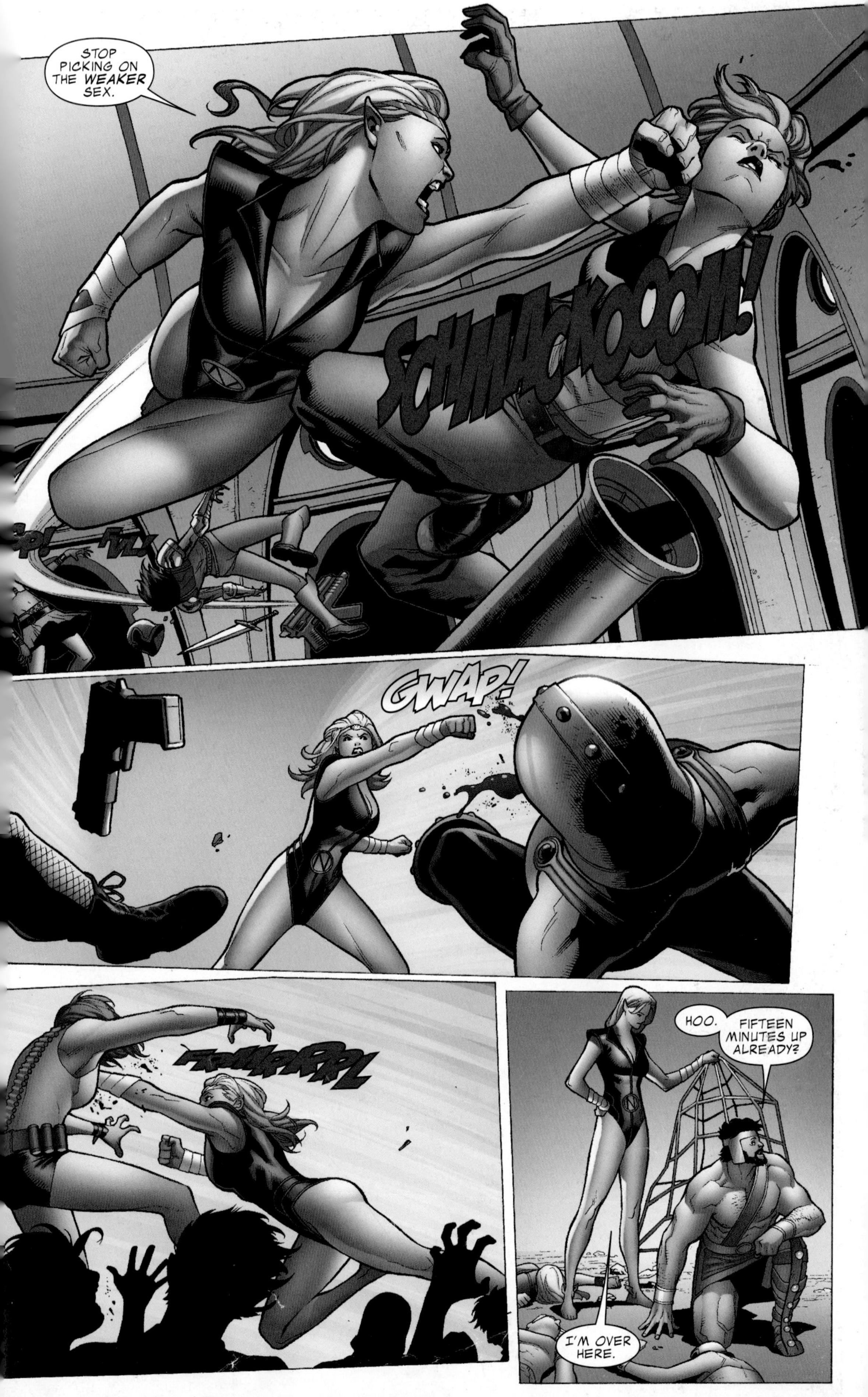
STOP PICKING ON THE WEAKER SEX.
SCHWACKOOOM!
GWAP!
HOO.
FIFTEEN MINUTES UP ALREADY?
I'M OVER HERE.

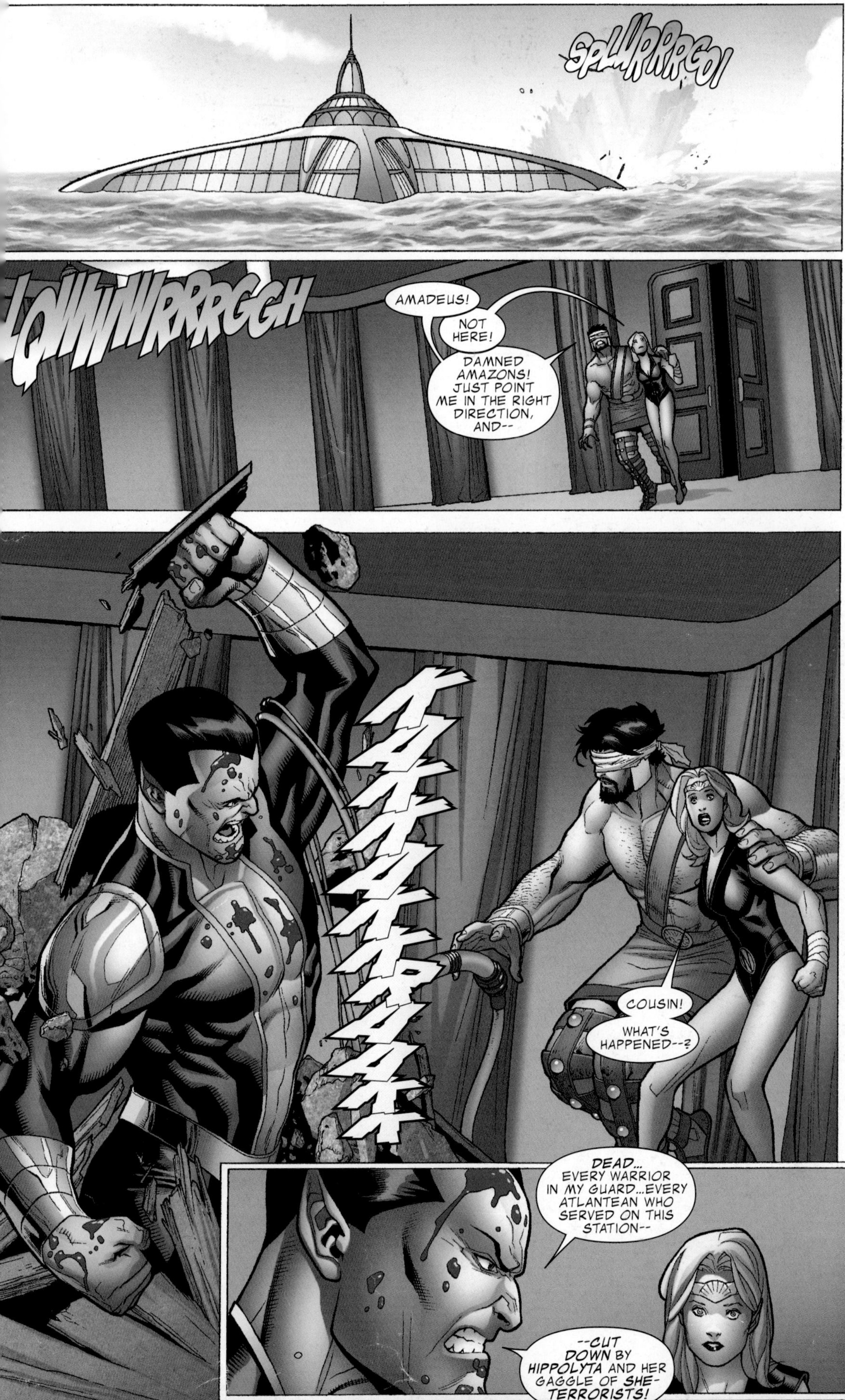
SPLURRRRGO!
LOWWWRRRGGH
AMADEUS!
NOT HERE!
DAMNED AMAZONS! JUST POINT ME IN THE RIGHT DIRECTION, AND--
COUSIN!
WHAT'S HAPPENED--?
DEAD... EVERY WARRIOR IN MY GUARD...EVERY ATLANTEAN WHO SERVED ON THIS STATION--
--CUT DOWN BY HIPPOLYTA AND HER GAGGLE OF SHE-TERRORISTS!

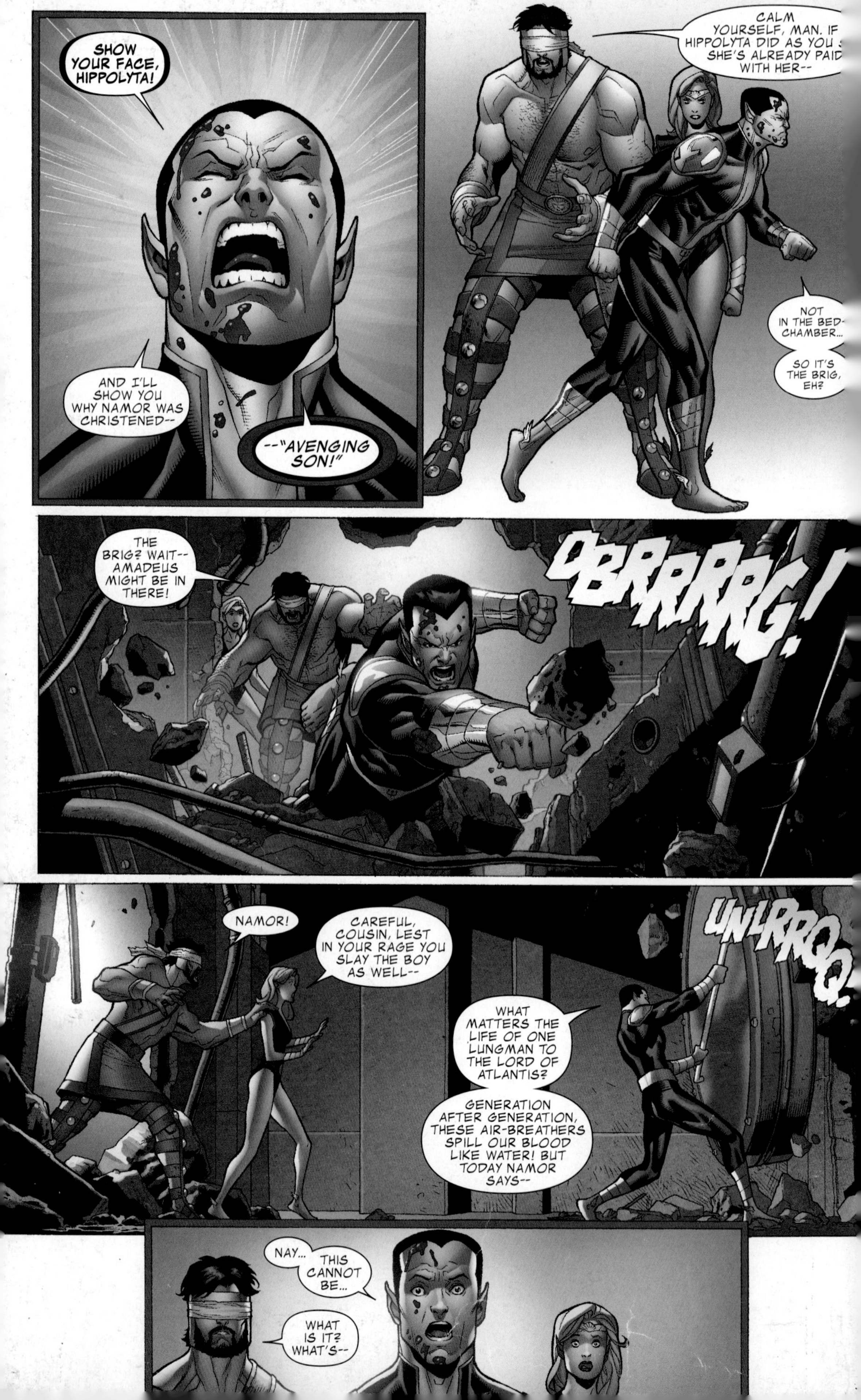
SHOW YOUR FACE, HIPPOLYTA!
AND I'LL SHOW YOU WHY NAMOR WAS CHRISTENED--
--"AVENGING SON!"
CALM YOURSELF, MAN. IF HIPPOLYTA DID AS YOU SHE'S ALREADY PAID WITH HER--
NOT IN THE BED-CHAMBER...
SO IT'S THE BRIG, EH?
THE BRIG? WAIT-- AMADEUS MIGHT BE IN THERE!
OBRRRRG!
NAMOR!
CAREFUL, COUSIN, LEST IN YOUR RAGE YOU SLAY THE BOY AS WELL--
UNLRRQQ.
WHAT MATTERS THE LIFE OF ONE LUNGMAN TO THE LORD OF ATLANTIS?
GENERATION AFTER GENERATION, THESE AIR-BREATHERS SPILL OUR BLOOD LIKE WATER! BUT TODAY NAMOR SAYS--
NAY... THIS CANNOT BE...
WHAT IS IT? WHAT'S--

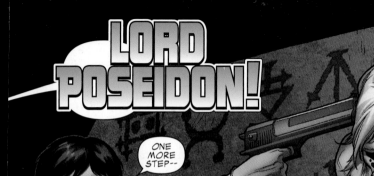

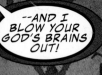

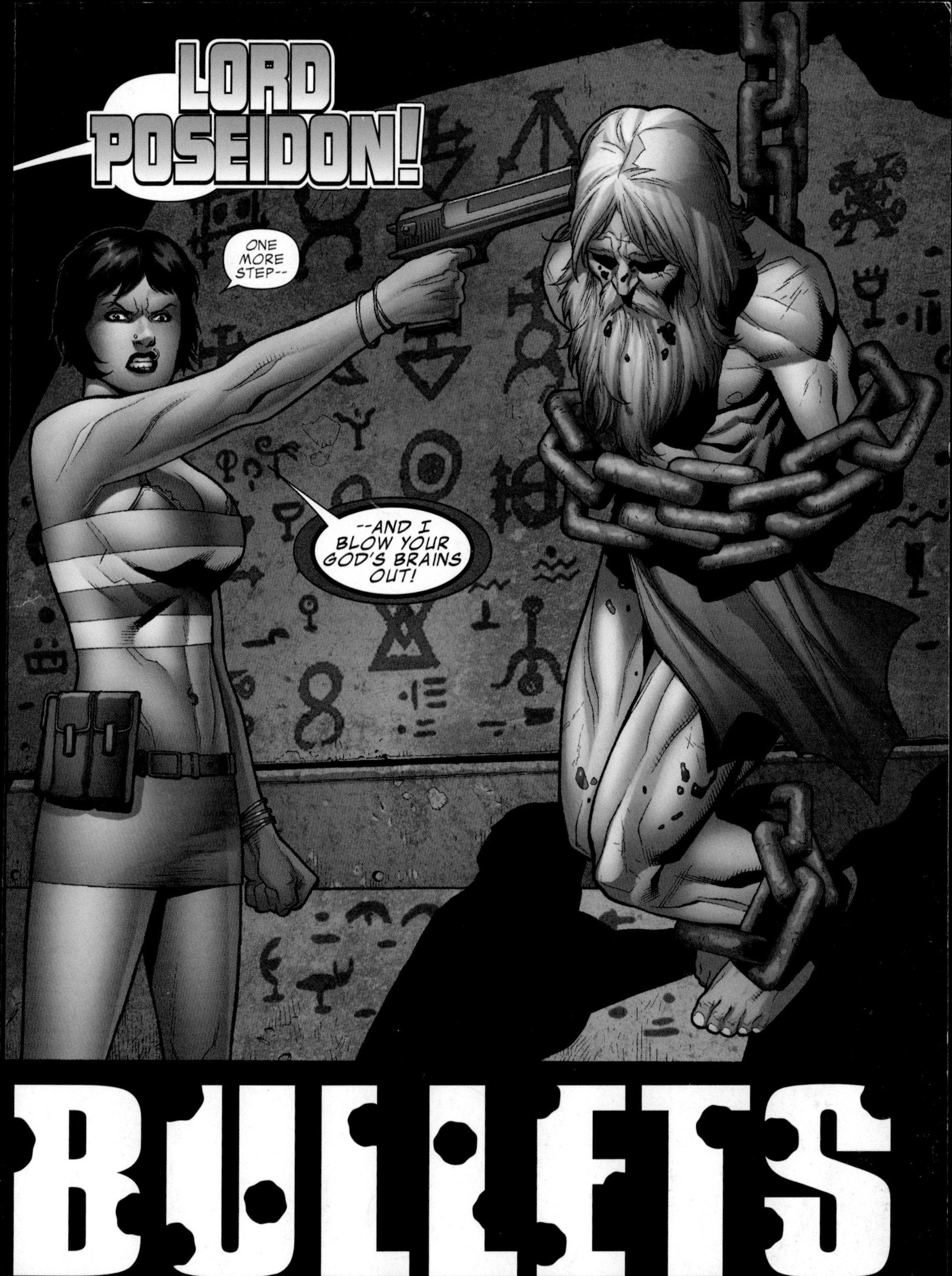
LORD POSEIDON!
ONE MORE STEP--
--AND I BLOW YOUR GOD'S BRAINS OUT!

# BULLETS & BRACELETS

PART TWO OF LOVE & WAR

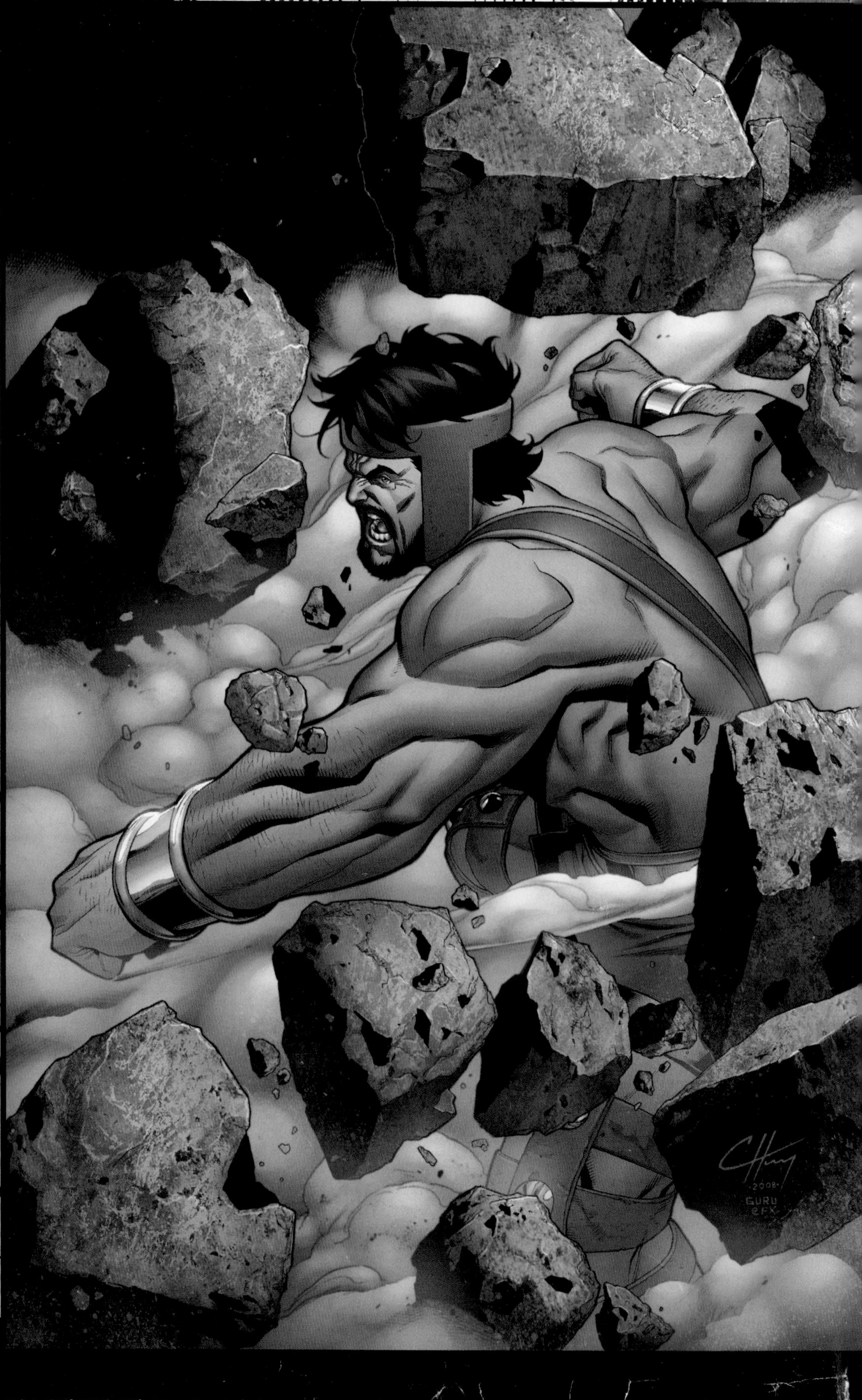
2008
GURU
eFX

INCREDIBLE HERCULES #123

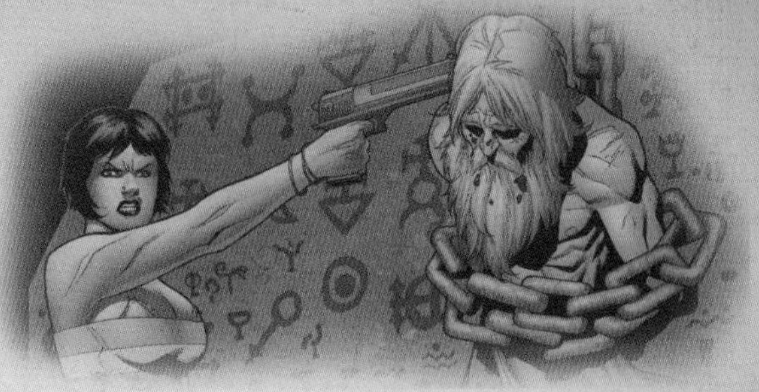

## O POSEIDON WITH LOVE

y ~~Anonymous,~~ Anonmadeus Cho

that's got a gun to his watery noggin...

begin to sing about Poseidon, the great god,

(I thought I'd be bearing some fruit, but the crazy-hot Amazons that wanted to breed with me...didn't actually want to breed with me)

nover of the earth and fruitless sea,

Namor & Namora

od of ~~the deep~~ who is also lord of Helicon and wide Aegae.

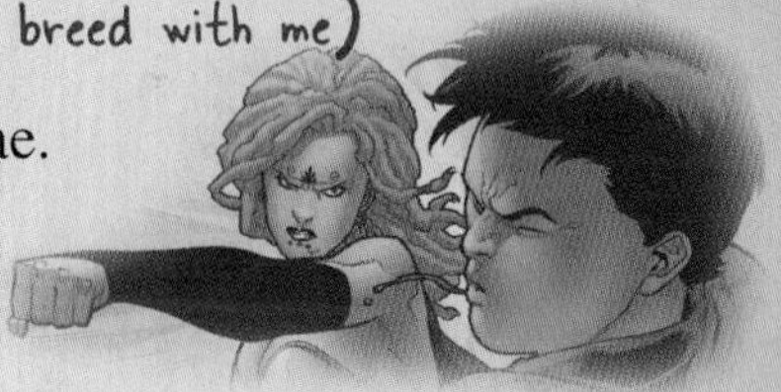

two-fold office the gods allotted you, O Shaker of Earth, to be a amer of horses and ~~a saviour of ships~~!

Herc's uncle. Guess what? Herc can't see (which sucks when all you're fighting is Amazonian babeishness)

Hail, Poseidon, Holder of the Earth, ~~dark-haired~~ blue-skinned lord!

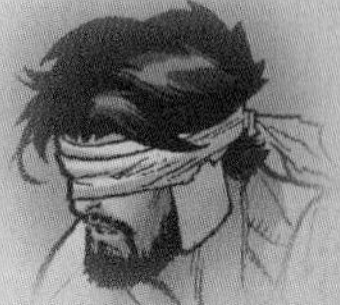

O blessed one, be kindly in heart and help those who voyage in ships!

and if you've got a second maybe save me from the psycho-femmes that won't give me any candy...

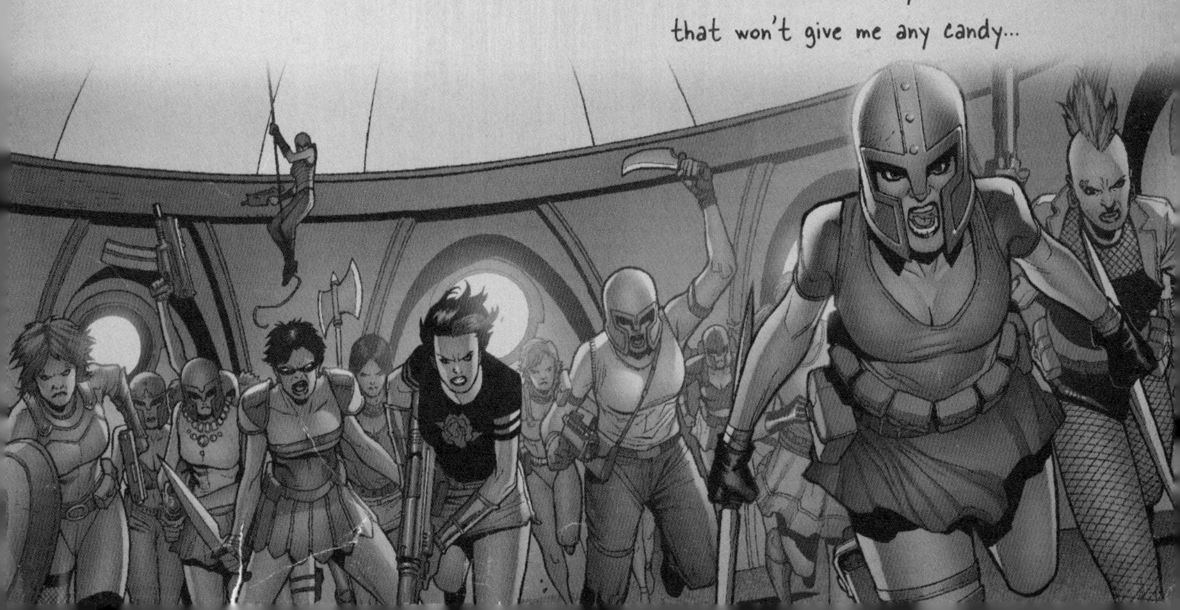

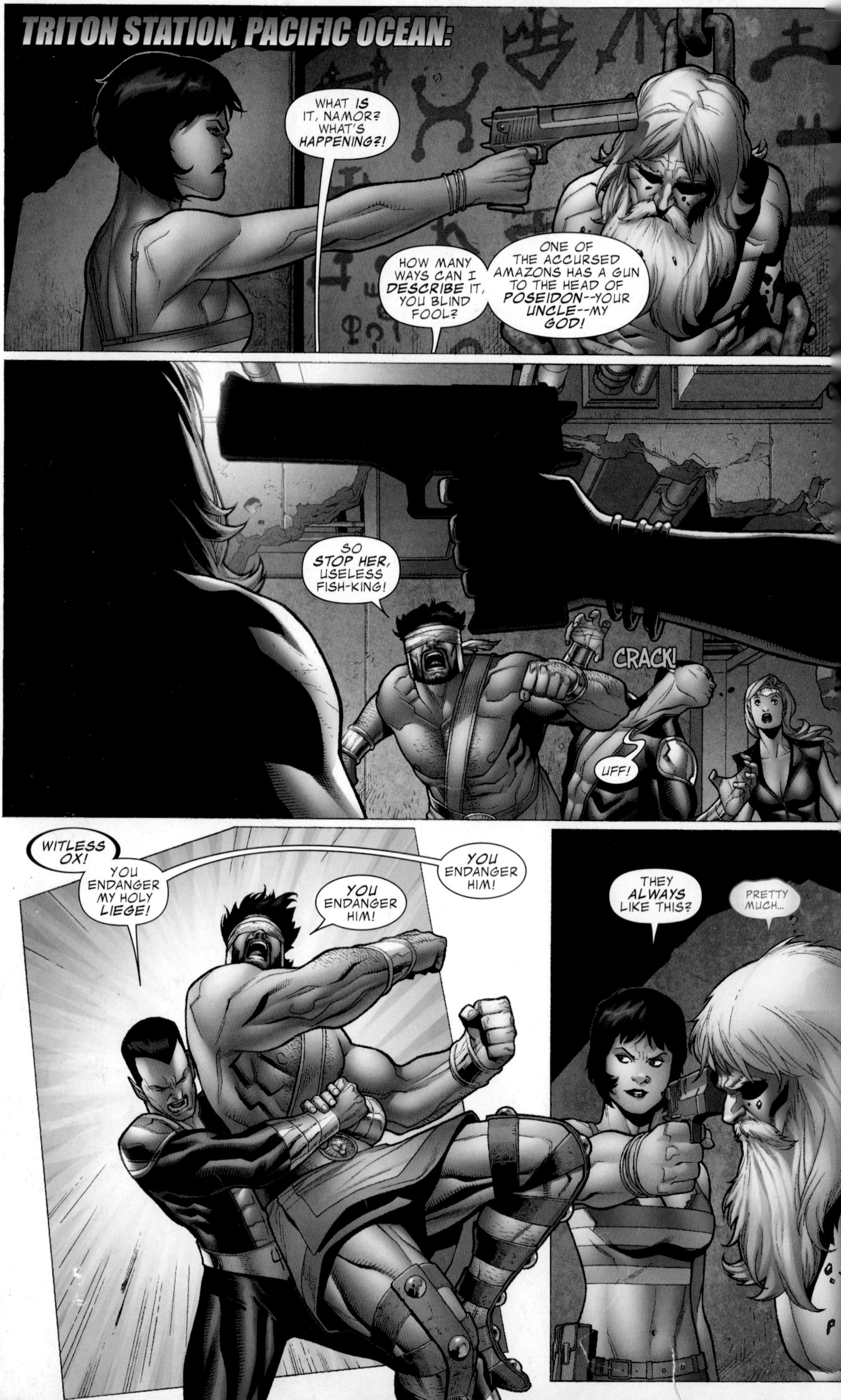
TRITON STATION, PACIFIC OCEAN:
WHAT IS IT, NAMOR? WHAT'S HAPPENING?!
HOW MANY WAYS CAN I DESCRIBE IT, YOU BLIND FOOL?
ONE OF THE ACCURSED AMAZONS HAS A GUN TO THE HEAD OF POSEIDON--YOUR UNCLE--MY GOD!
SO STOP HER, USELESS FISH-KING!
CRACK!
UFF!
WITLESS OX!
YOU ENDANGER MY HOLY LIEGE!
YOU ENDANGER HIM!
YOU ENDANGER HIM!
THEY ALWAYS LIKE THIS?
PRETTY MUCH...

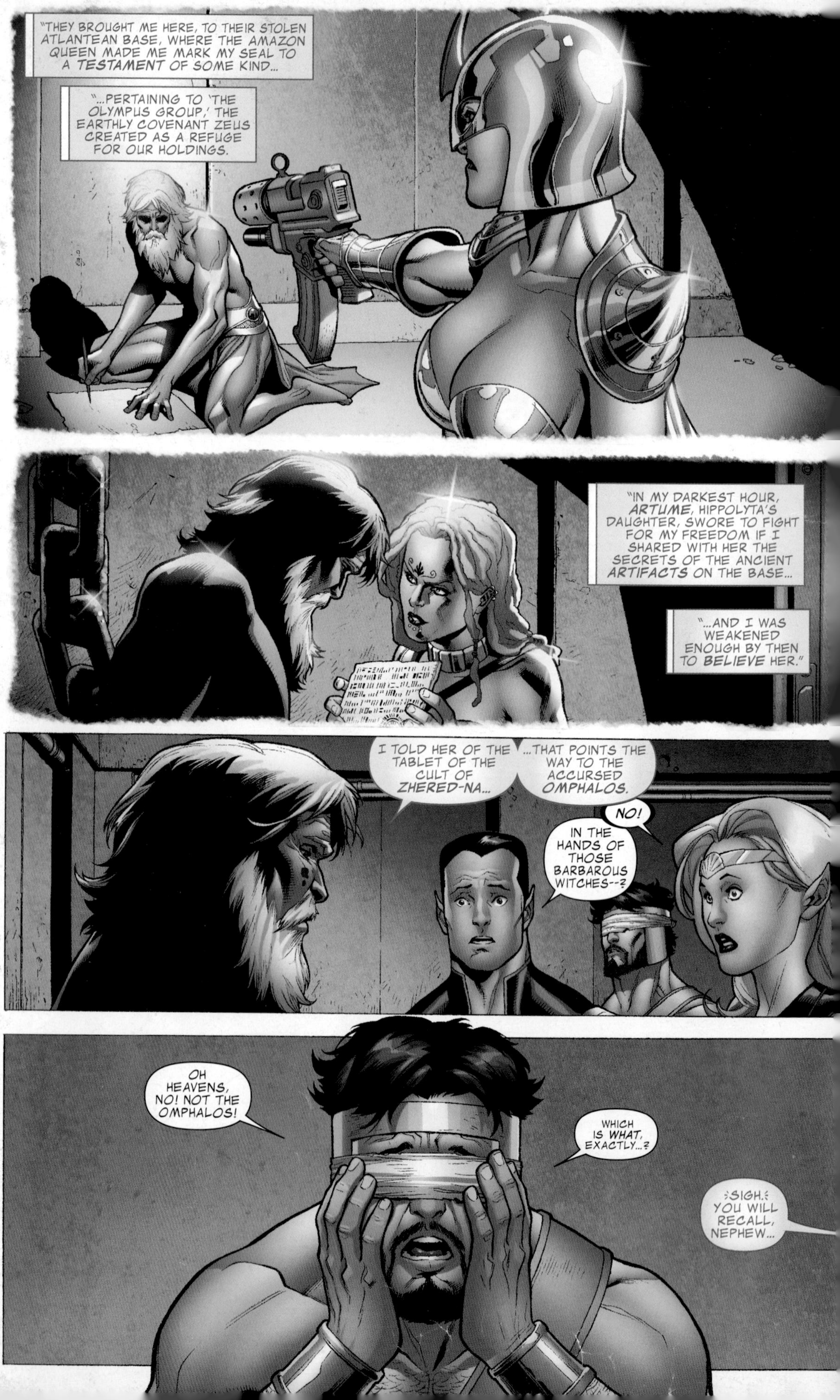
"THEY BROUGHT ME HERE, TO THEIR STOLEN ATLANTEAN BASE, WHERE THE AMAZON QUEEN MADE ME MARK MY SEAL TO A TESTAMENT OF SOME KIND...
"...PERTAINING TO 'THE OLYMPUS GROUP,' THE EARTHLY COVENANT ZEUS CREATED AS A REFUGE FOR OUR HOLDINGS.
"IN MY DARKEST HOUR, ARTUME, HIPPOLYTA'S DAUGHTER, SWORE TO FIGHT FOR MY FREEDOM IF I SHARED WITH HER THE SECRETS OF THE ANCIENT ARTIFACTS ON THE BASE...
"...AND I WAS WEAKENED ENOUGH BY THEN TO BELIEVE HER."
I TOLD HER OF THE TABLET OF THE CULT OF ZHERED-NA...
...THAT POINTS THE WAY TO THE ACCURSED OMPHALOS.
NO!
IN THE HANDS OF THOSE BARBAROUS WITCHES--?
OH HEAVENS, NO! NOT THE OMPHALOS!
WHICH IS WHAT, EXACTLY...?
SIGH. YOU WILL RECALL, NEPHEW...

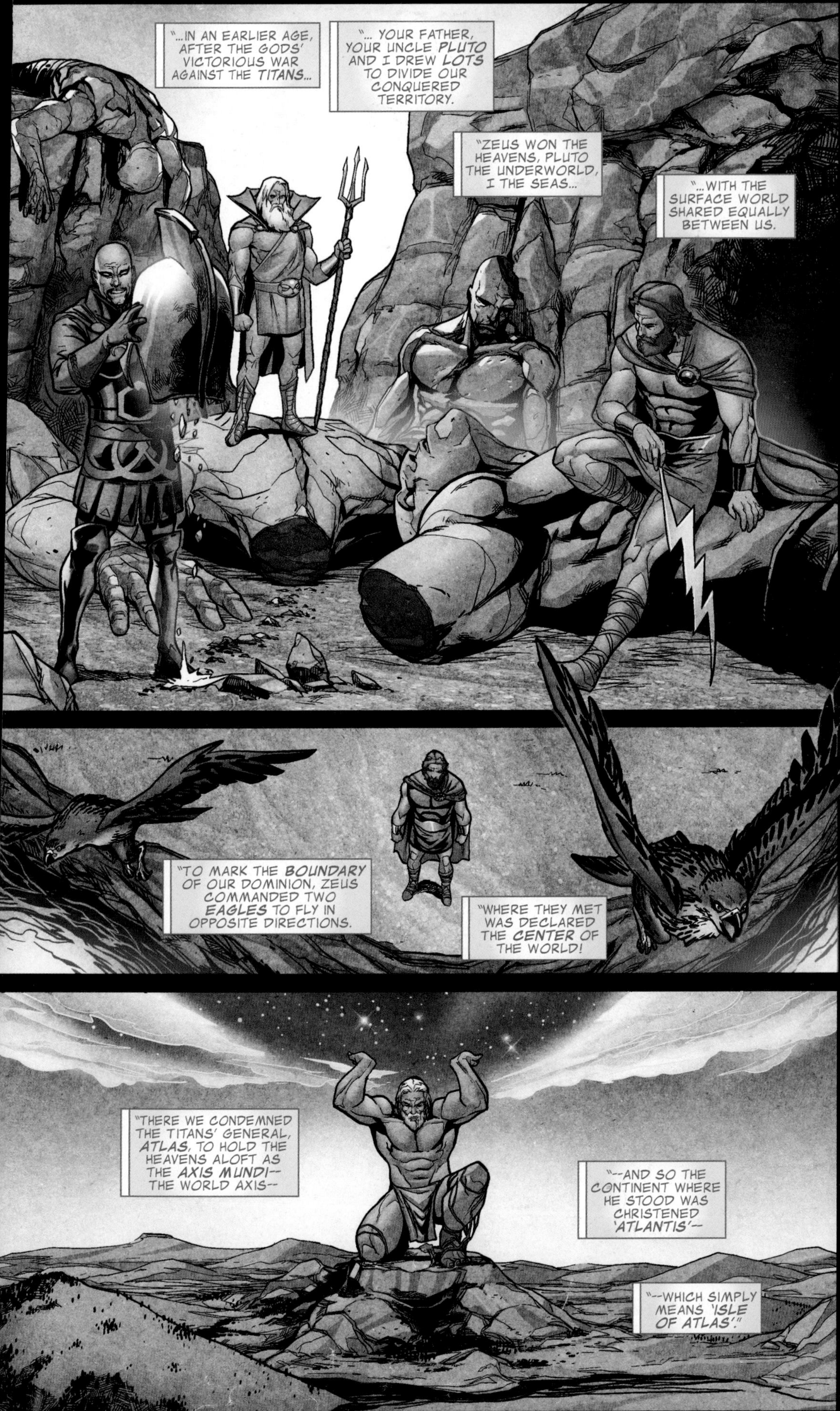
"...IN AN EARLIER AGE, AFTER THE GODS' VICTORIOUS WAR AGAINST THE TITANS...
"... YOUR FATHER, YOUR UNCLE PLUTO AND I DREW LOTS TO DIVIDE OUR CONQUERED TERRITORY.
"ZEUS WON THE HEAVENS, PLUTO THE UNDERWORLD, I THE SEAS...
"...WITH THE SURFACE WORLD SHARED EQUALLY BETWEEN US.
"TO MARK THE BOUNDARY OF OUR DOMINION, ZEUS COMMANDED TWO EAGLES TO FLY IN OPPOSITE DIRECTIONS.
"WHERE THEY MET WAS DECLARED THE CENTER OF THE WORLD!
"THERE WE CONDEMNED THE TITANS' GENERAL, ATLAS, TO HOLD THE HEAVENS ALOFT AS THE AXIS MUNDI-- THE WORLD AXIS--
"--AND SO THE CONTINENT WHERE HE STOOD WAS CHRISTENED 'ATLANTIS'--
"--WHICH SIMPLY MEANS 'ISLE OF ATLAS'."

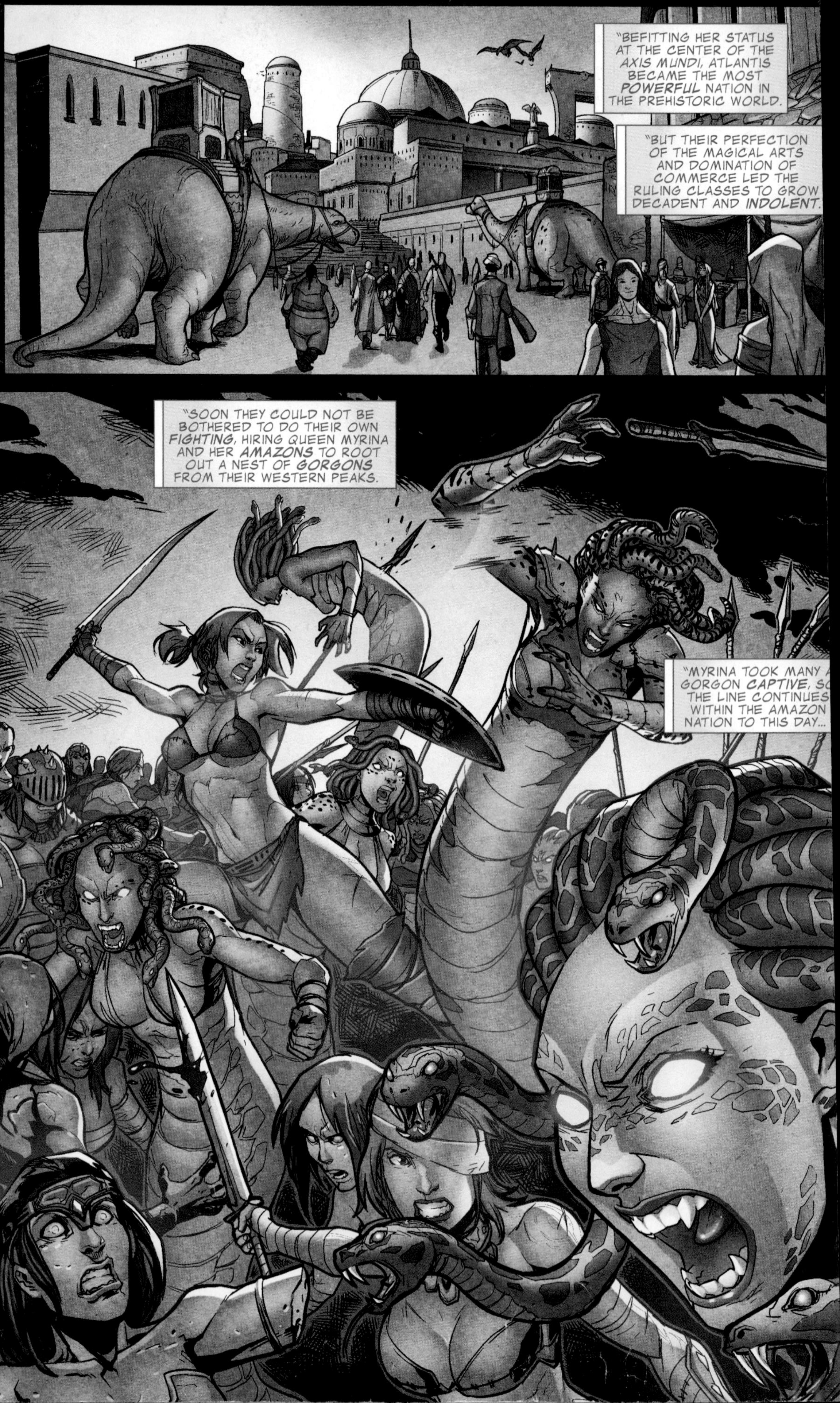
"BEFITTING HER STATUS AT THE CENTER OF THE AXIS MUNDI, ATLANTIS BECAME THE MOST POWERFUL NATION IN THE PREHISTORIC WORLD.
"BUT THEIR PERFECTION OF THE MAGICAL ARTS AND DOMINATION OF COMMERCE LED THE RULING CLASSES TO GROW DECADENT AND INDOLENT.
"SOON THEY COULD NOT BE BOTHERED TO DO THEIR OWN FIGHTING, HIRING QUEEN MYRINA AND HER AMAZONS TO ROOT OUT A NEST OF GORGONS FROM THEIR WESTERN PEAKS.
"MYRINA TOOK MANY A GORGON CAPTIVE, SO THE LINE CONTINUES WITHIN THE AMAZON NATION TO THIS DAY...

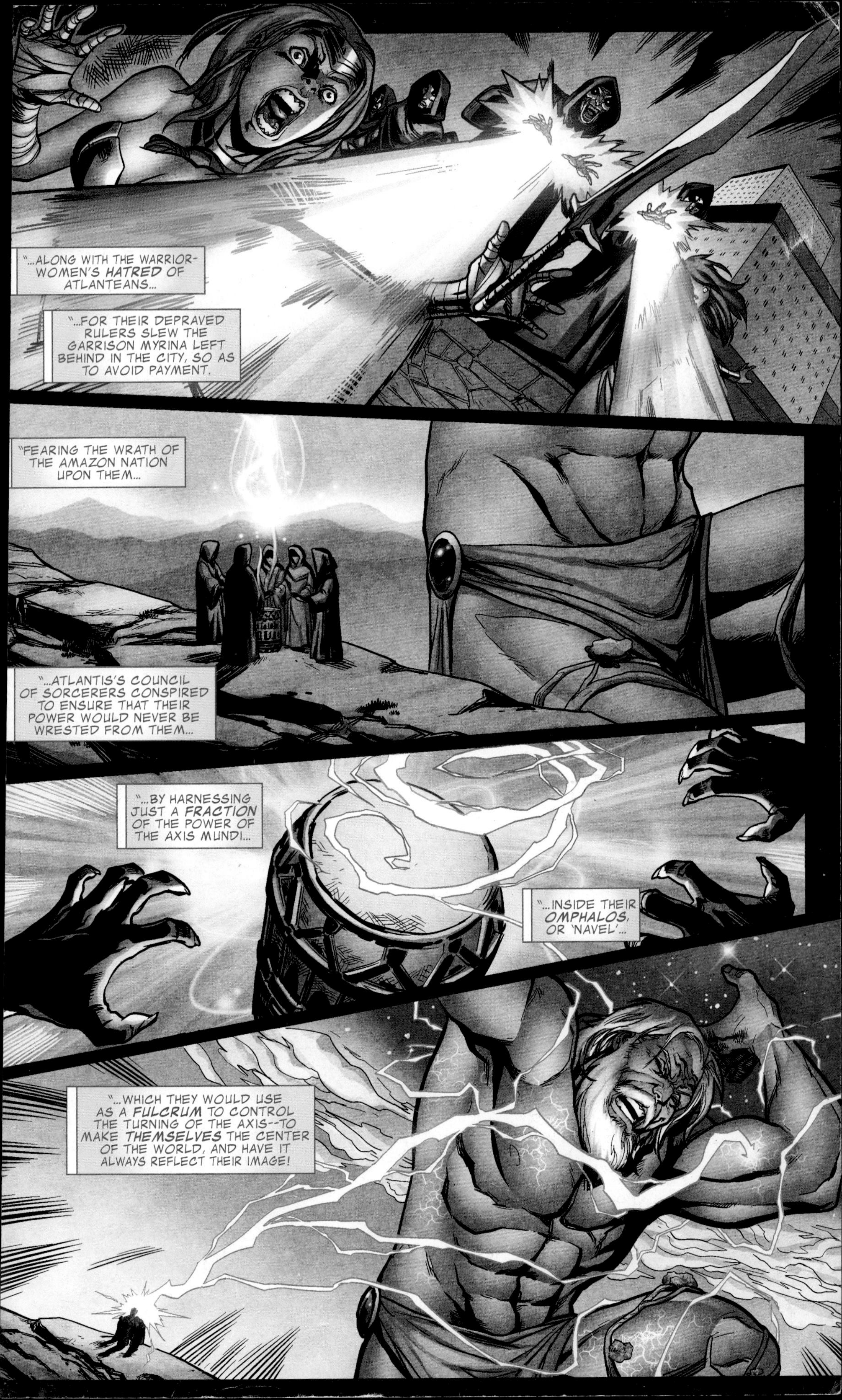
"...ALONG WITH THE WARRIOR-WOMEN'S HATRED OF ATLANTEANS...
"...FOR THEIR DEPRAVED RULERS SLEW THE GARRISON MYRINA LEFT BEHIND IN THE CITY, SO AS TO AVOID PAYMENT.
"FEARING THE WRATH OF THE AMAZON NATION UPON THEM...
"...ATLANTIS'S COUNCIL OF SORCERERS CONSPIRED TO ENSURE THAT THEIR POWER WOULD NEVER BE WRESTED FROM THEM...
"...BY HARNESSING JUST A FRACTION OF THE POWER OF THE AXIS MUNDI...
"...INSIDE THEIR OMPHALOS, OR 'NAVEL'...
"...WHICH THEY WOULD USE AS A FULCRUM TO CONTROL THE TURNING OF THE AXIS--TO MAKE THEMSELVES THE CENTER OF THE WORLD, AND HAVE IT ALWAYS REFLECT THEIR IMAGE!

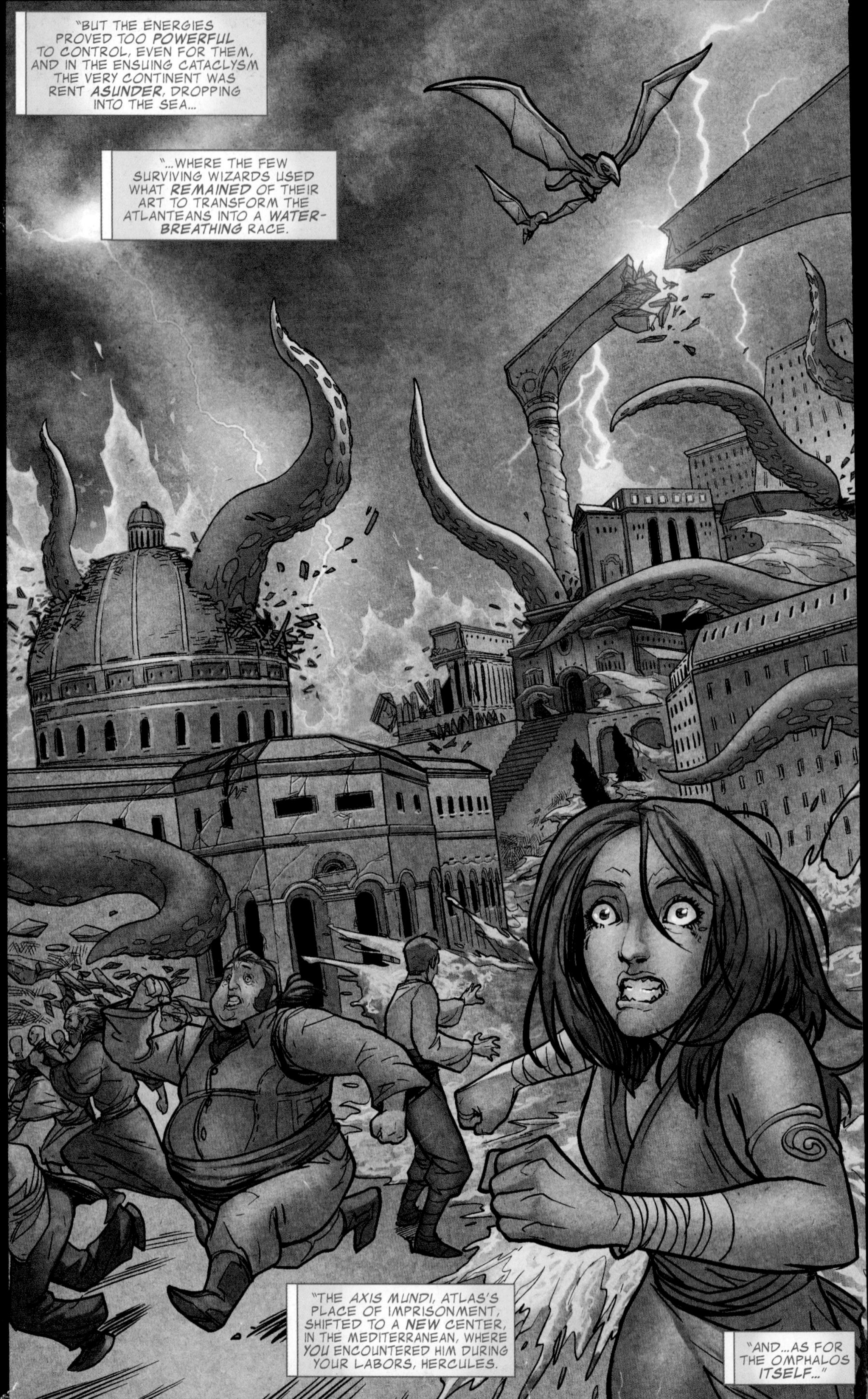
"BUT THE ENERGIES PROVED TOO POWERFUL TO CONTROL, EVEN FOR THEM, AND IN THE ENSUING CATACLYSM THE VERY CONTINENT WAS RENT ASUNDER, DROPPING INTO THE SEA...
"...WHERE THE FEW SURVIVING WIZARDS USED WHAT REMAINED OF THEIR ART TO TRANSFORM THE ATLANTEANS INTO A WATER-BREATHING RACE.
"THE AXIS MUNDI, ATLAS'S PLACE OF IMPRISONMENT, SHIFTED TO A NEW CENTER, IN THE MEDITERRANEAN, WHERE YOU ENCOUNTERED HIM DURING YOUR LABORS, HERCULES.
"AND...AS FOR THE OMPHALOS ITSELF..."

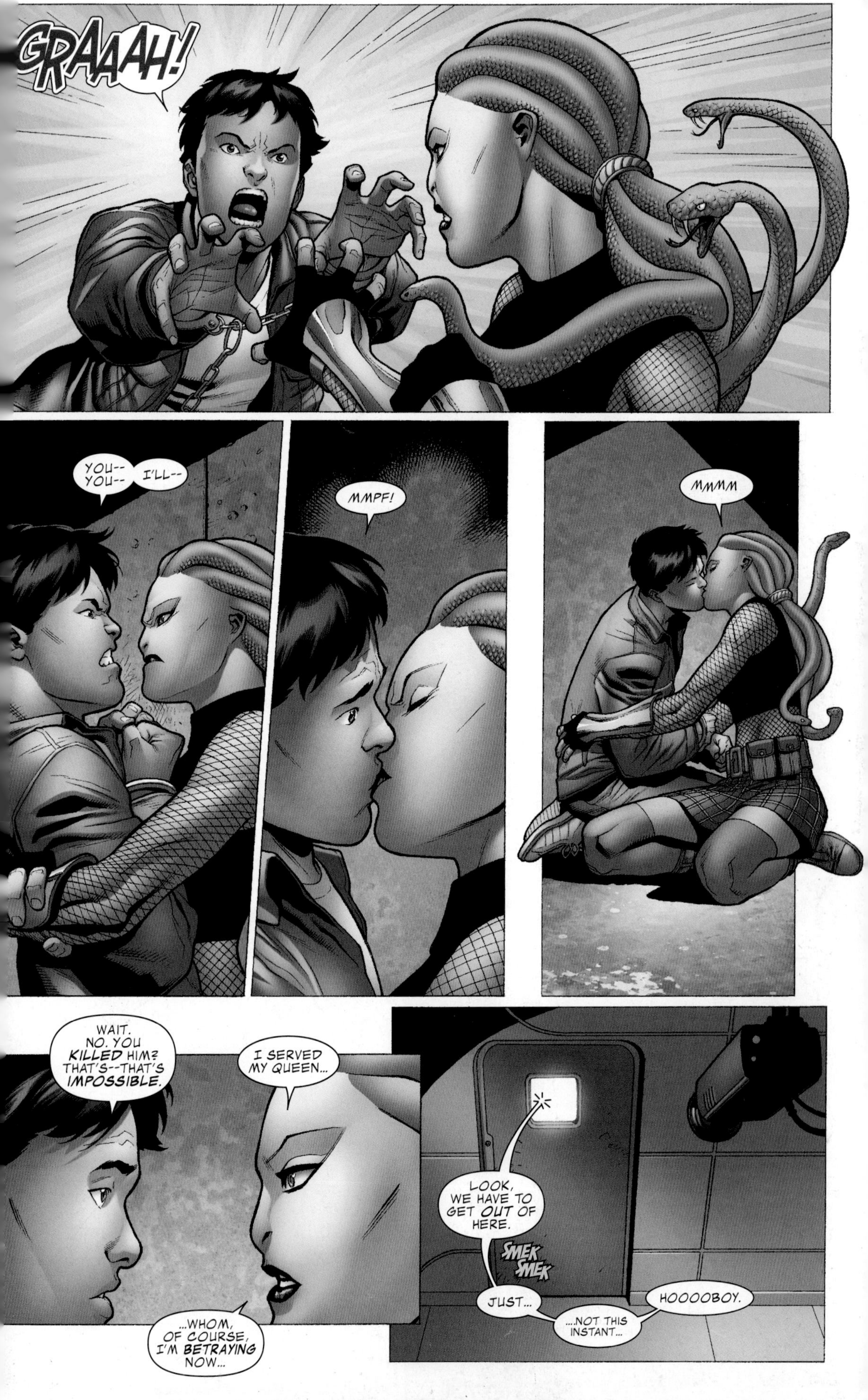
GRAAAH!
YOU-- YOU-- I'LL--
MMPF!
MMMM
WAIT. NO. YOU KILLED HIM? THAT'S--THAT'S IMPOSSIBLE.
I SERVED MY QUEEN...
...WHOM, OF COURSE, I'M BETRAYING NOW...
LOOK, WE HAVE TO GET OUT OF HERE.
SMEK SMEK
JUST...
...NOT THIS INSTANT...
HOOOOBOY.

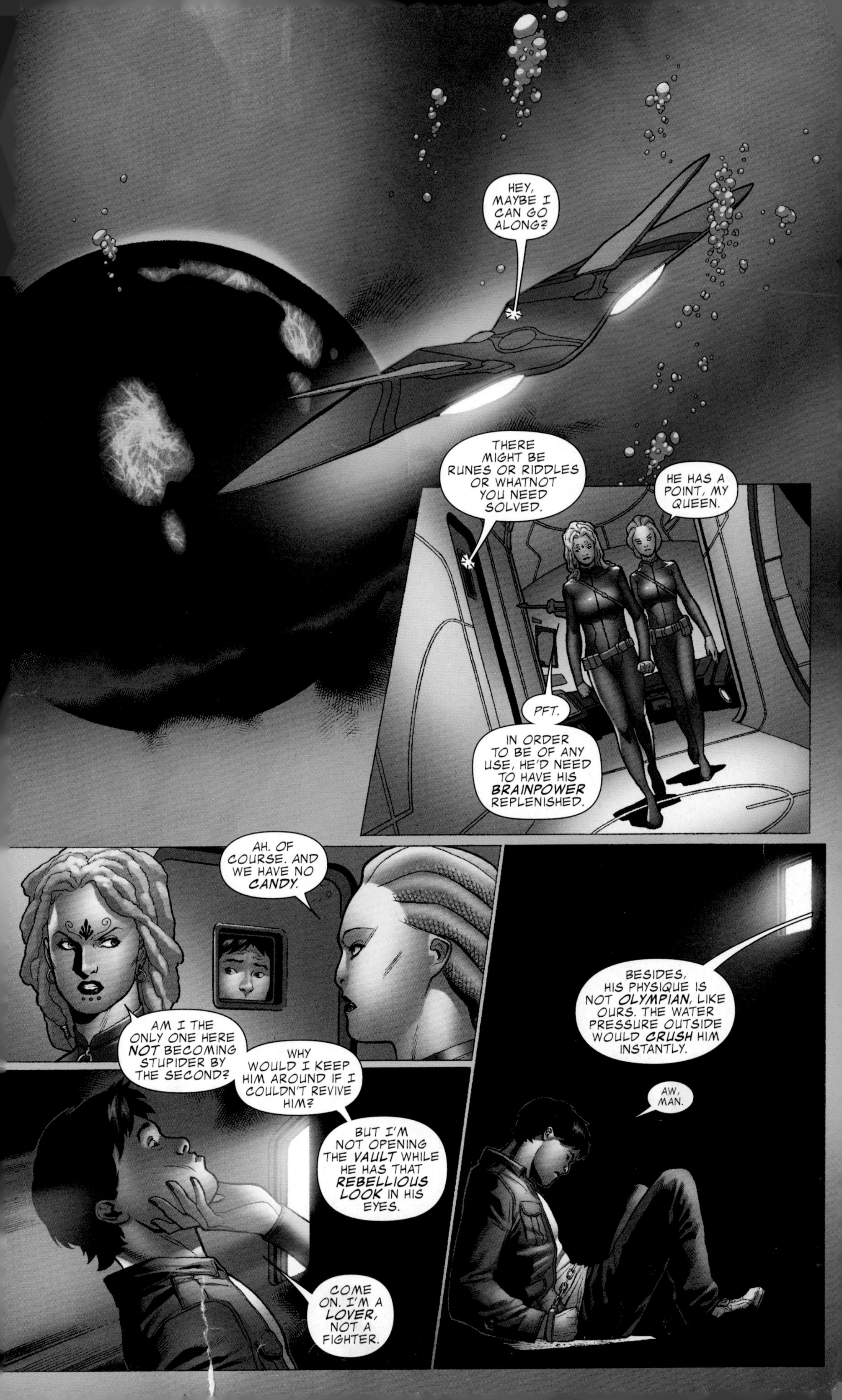

HEY, MAYBE I CAN GO ALONG?
THERE MIGHT BE RUNES OR RIDDLES OR WHATNOT YOU NEED SOLVED.
HE HAS A POINT, MY QUEEN.
PFT.
IN ORDER TO BE OF ANY USE, HE'D NEED TO HAVE HIS BRAINPOWER REPLENISHED.
AH. OF COURSE. AND WE HAVE NO CANDY.
AM I THE ONLY ONE HERE NOT BECOMING STUPIDER BY THE SECOND?
WHY WOULD I KEEP HIM AROUND IF I COULDN'T REVIVE HIM?
BUT I'M NOT OPENING THE VAULT WHILE HE HAS THAT REBELLIOUS LOOK IN HIS EYES.
COME ON. I'M A LOVER, NOT A FIGHTER.
BESIDES, HIS PHYSIQUE IS NOT OLYMPIAN, LIKE OURS. THE WATER PRESSURE OUTSIDE WOULD CRUSH HIM INSTANTLY.
AW, MAN.

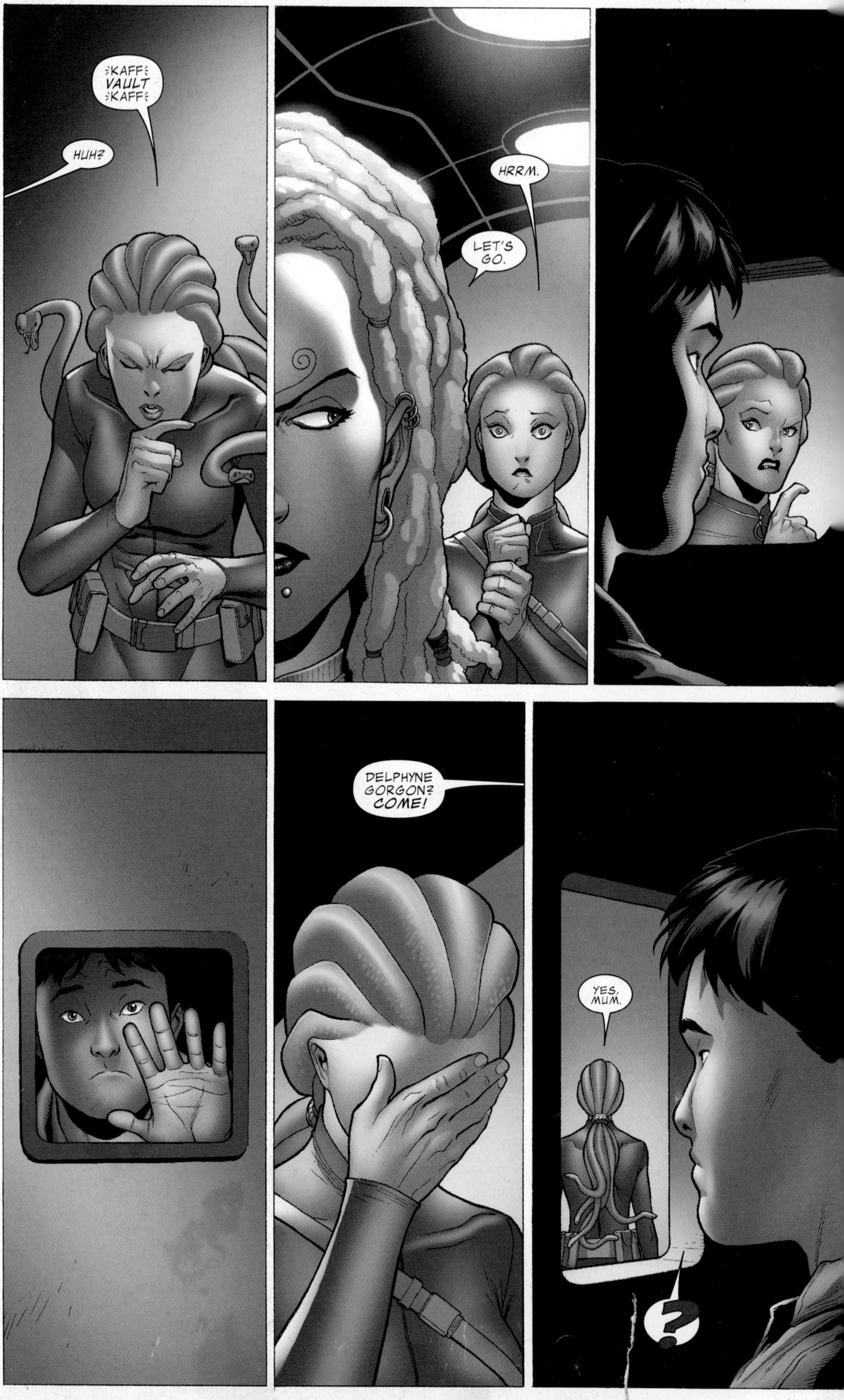
KAFF VAULT KAFF
HUH?
HRRM.
LET'S GO.
DELPHYNE GORGON? COME!
YES, MUM.
?

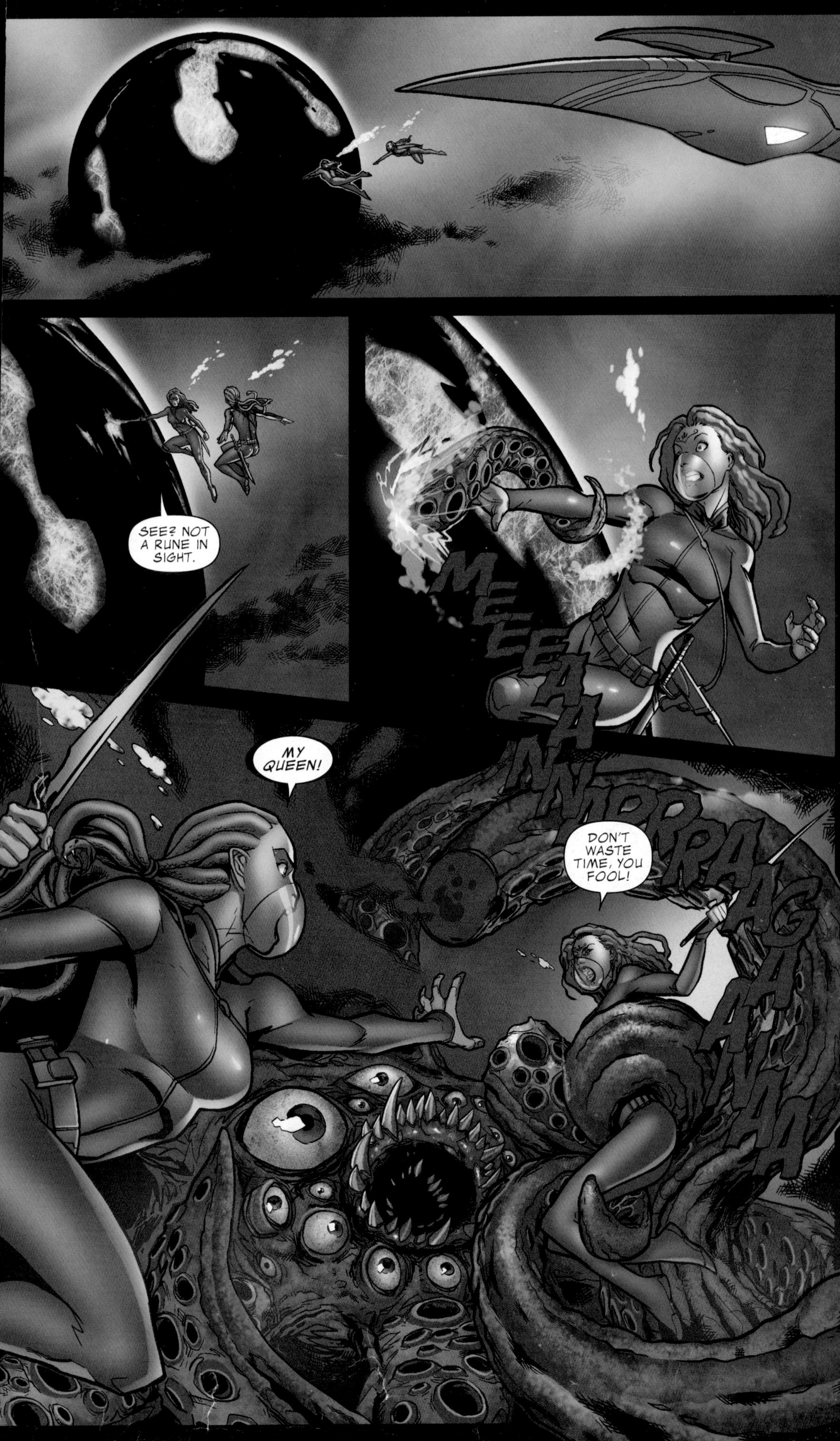

SEE? NOT A RUNE IN SIGHT.
MEEEAANNRRAAGAAAAA
MY QUEEN!
DON'T WASTE TIME, YOU FOOL!

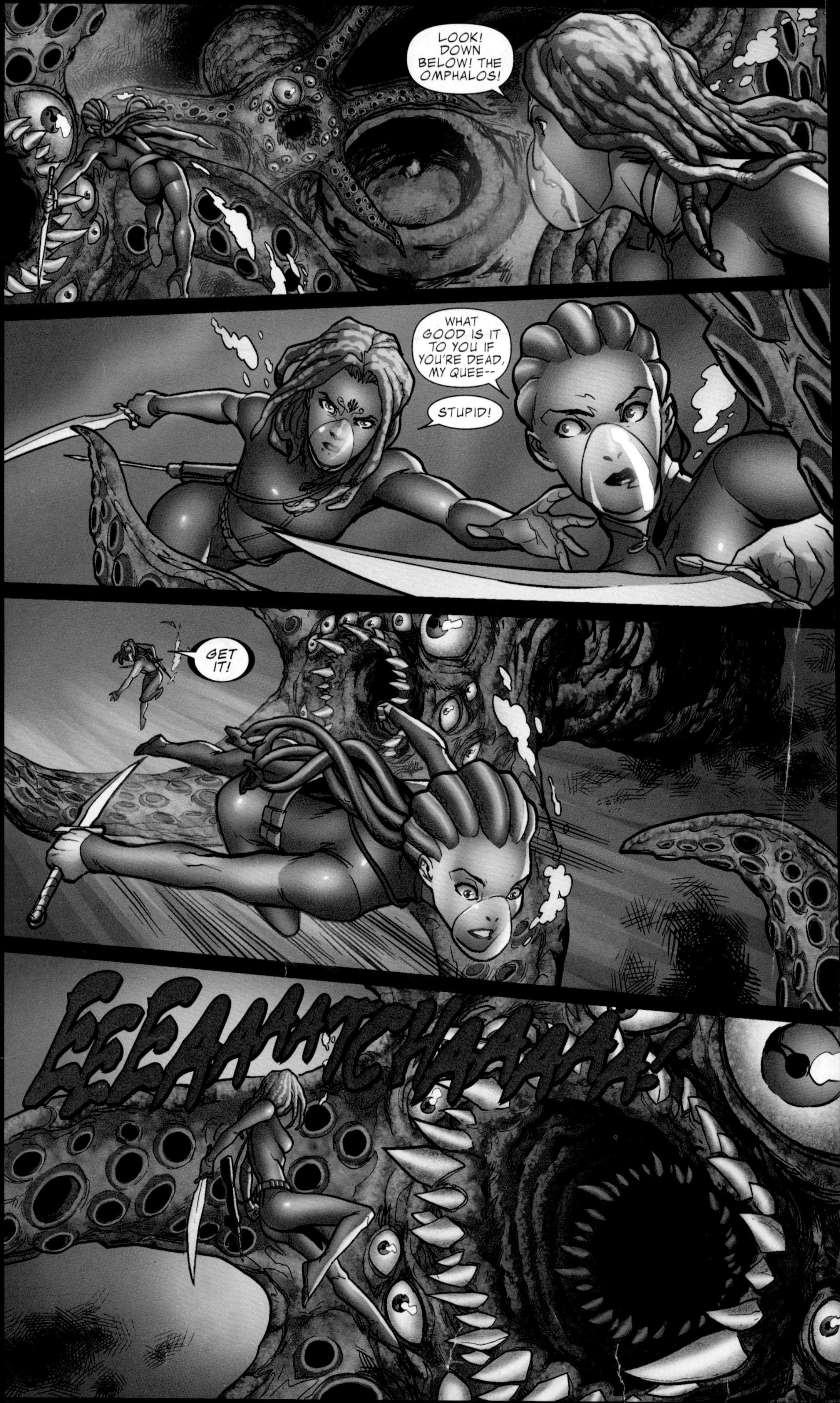
LOOK! DOWN BELOW! THE OMPHALOS!
WHAT GOOD IS IT TO YOU IF YOU'RE DEAD, MY QUEE--
STUPID!
GET IT!
EEEAAAHTCHAAAAA!

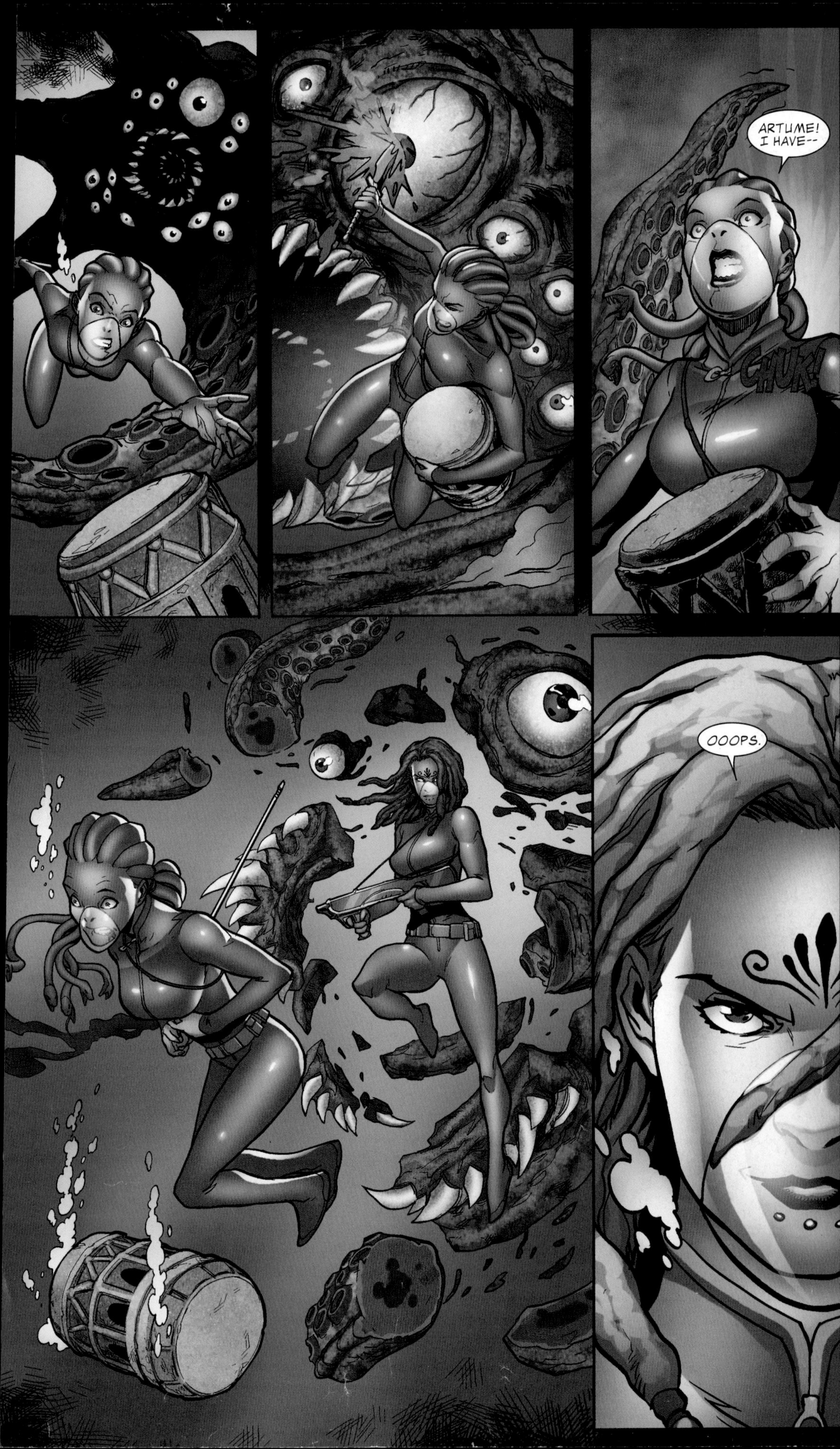
ARTUME! I HAVE--
CHUK!
OOOPS.

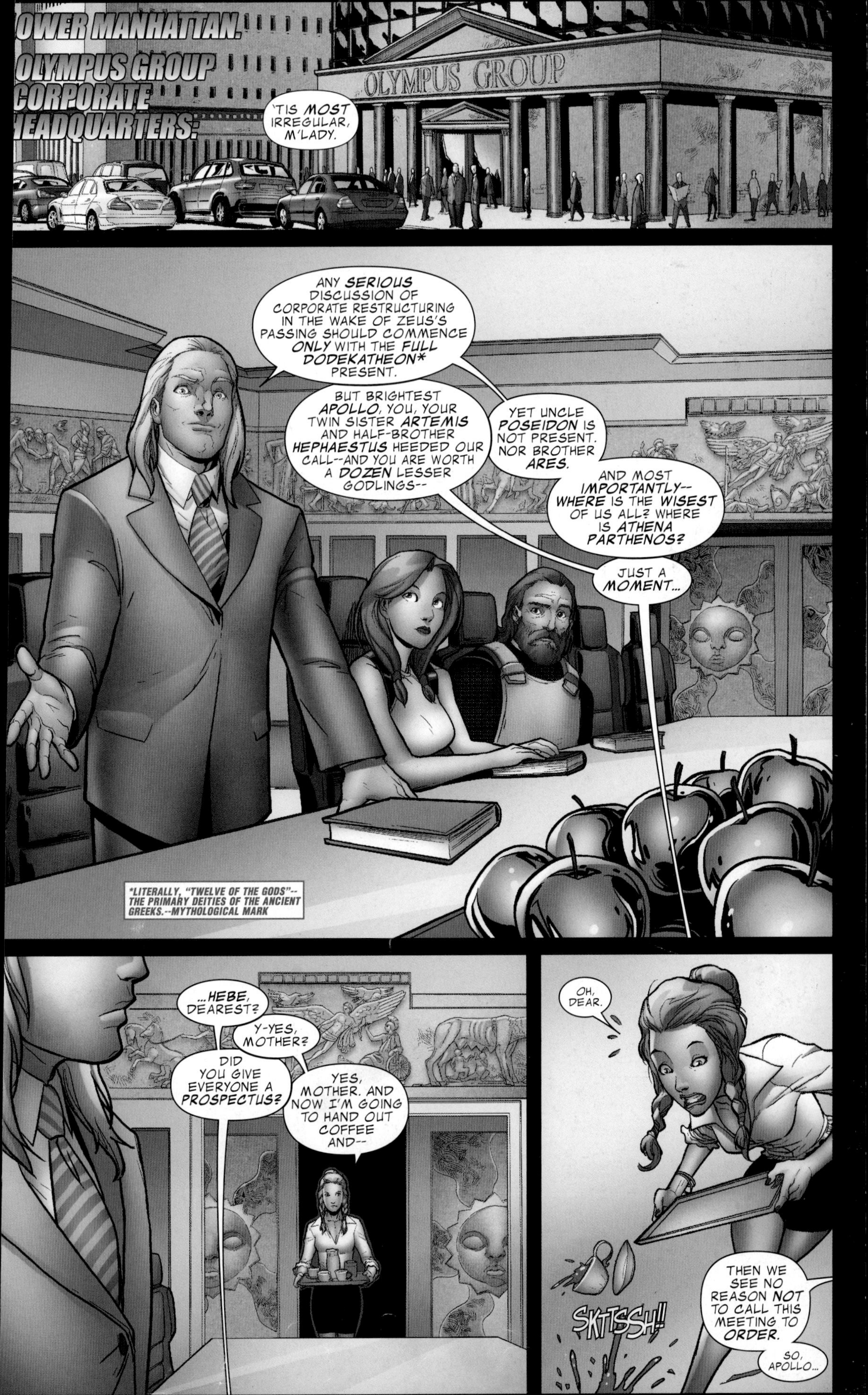
OWER MANHATTAN.
OLYMPUS GROUP CORPORATE HEADQUARTERS:
OLYMPUS GROUP
'TIS MOST IRREGULAR, M'LADY.
ANY SERIOUS DISCUSSION OF CORPORATE RESTRUCTURING IN THE WAKE OF ZEUS'S PASSING SHOULD COMMENCE ONLY WITH THE FULL DODEKATHEON* PRESENT.
BUT BRIGHTEST APOLLO, YOU, YOUR TWIN SISTER ARTEMIS AND HALF-BROTHER HEPHAESTUS HEEDED OUR CALL--AND YOU ARE WORTH A DOZEN LESSER GODLINGS--
YET UNCLE POSEIDON IS NOT PRESENT. NOR BROTHER ARES.
AND MOST IMPORTANTLY--WHERE IS THE WISEST OF US ALL? WHERE IS ATHENA PARTHENOS?
JUST A MOMENT...
*LITERALLY, "TWELVE OF THE GODS"--THE PRIMARY DEITIES OF THE ANCIENT GREEKS.--MYTHOLOGICAL MARK
...HEBE, DEAREST?
Y-YES, MOTHER?
DID YOU GIVE EVERYONE A PROSPECTUS?
YES, MOTHER. AND NOW I'M GOING TO HAND OUT COFFEE AND--
OH, DEAR.
SKTSSH!!
THEN WE SEE NO REASON NOT TO CALL THIS MEETING TO ORDER.
SO, APOLLO...

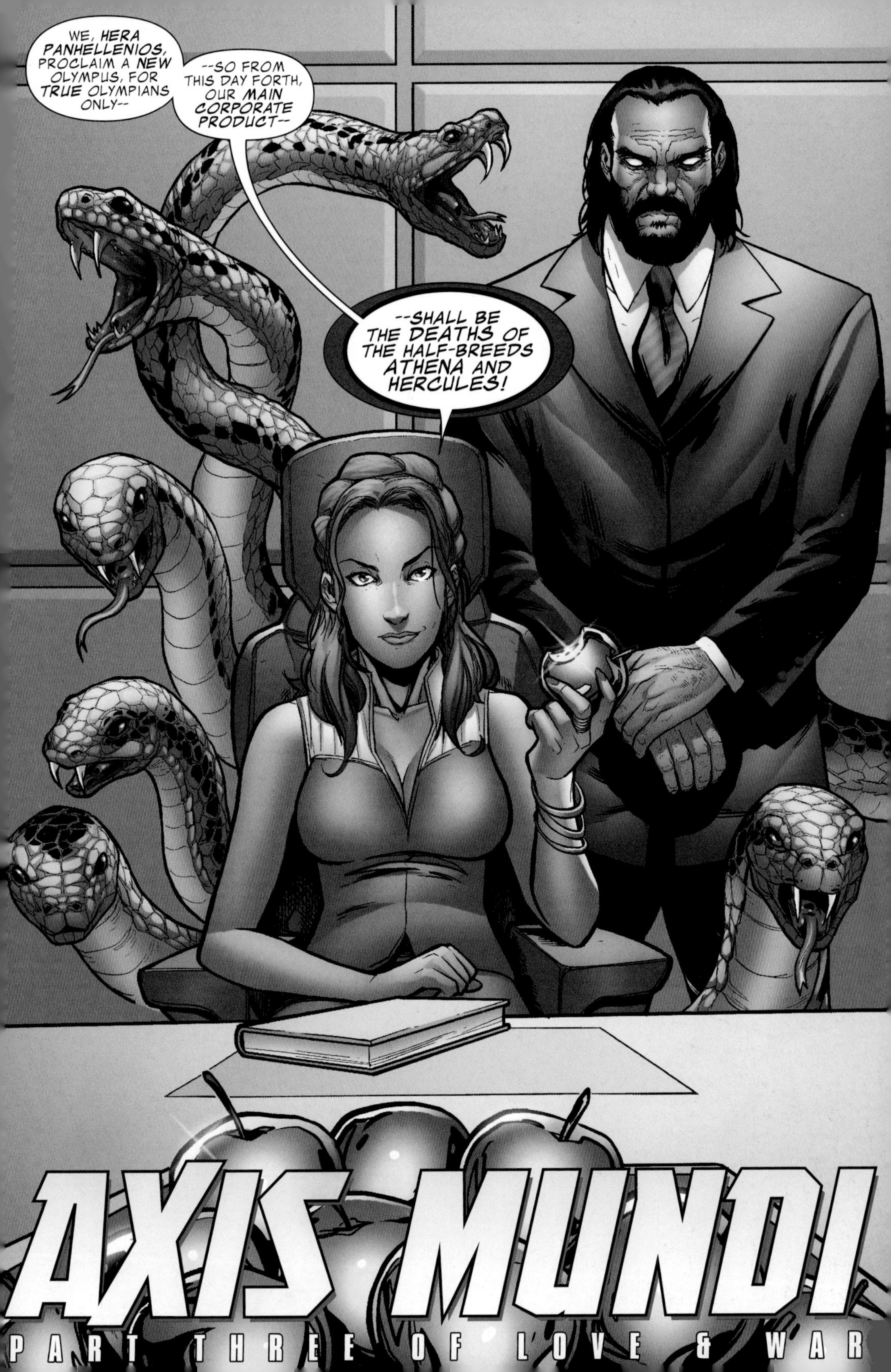
WE, HERA PANHELLENIOS, PROCLAIM A NEW OLYMPUS, FOR TRUE OLYMPIANS ONLY--
--SO FROM THIS DAY FORTH, OUR MAIN CORPORATE PRODUCT--
--SHALL BE THE DEATHS OF THE HALF-BREEDS ATHENA AND HERCULES!
AXIS MUNDI
PART THREE OF LOVE & WAR

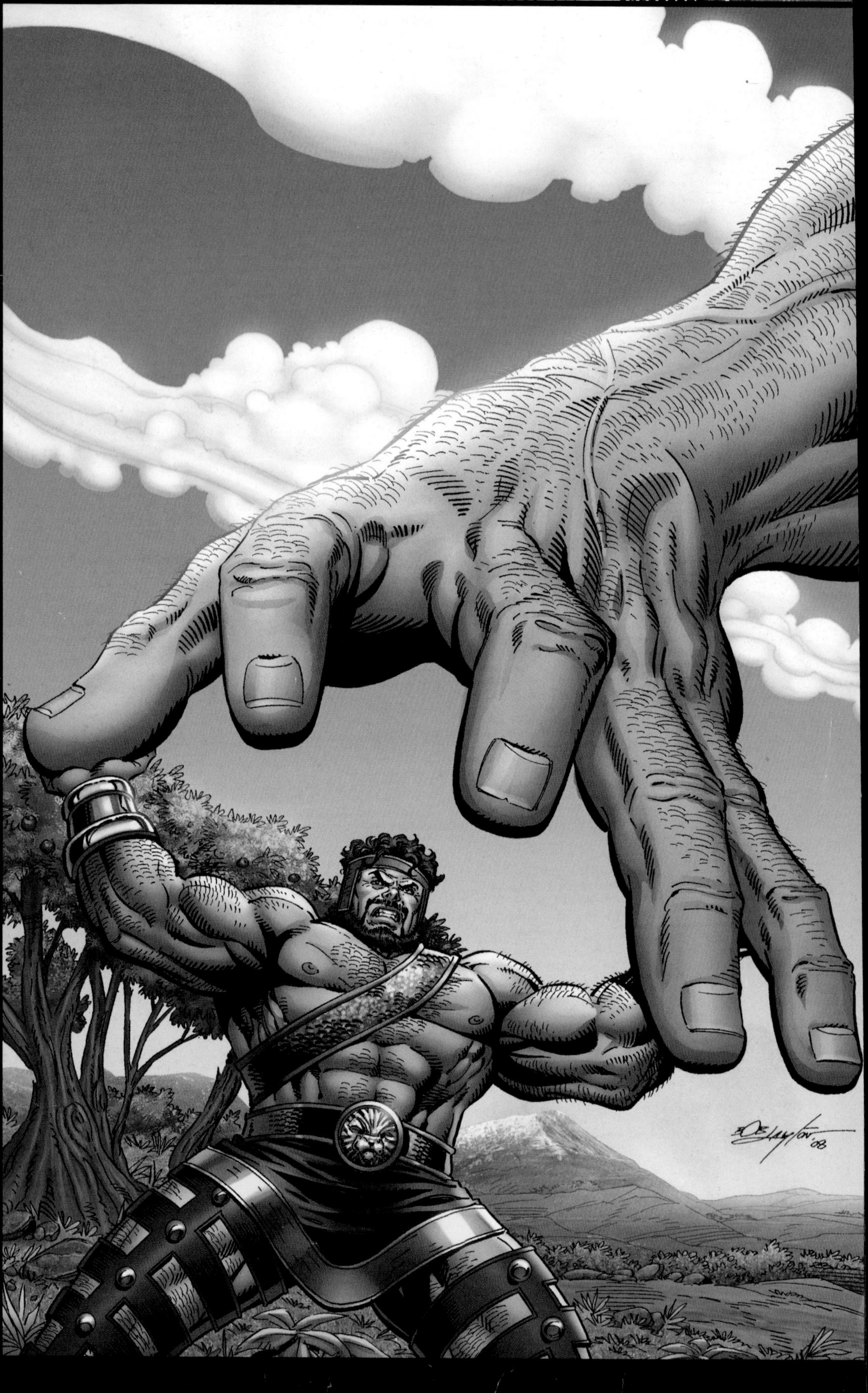

INCREDIBLE HERCULES #124

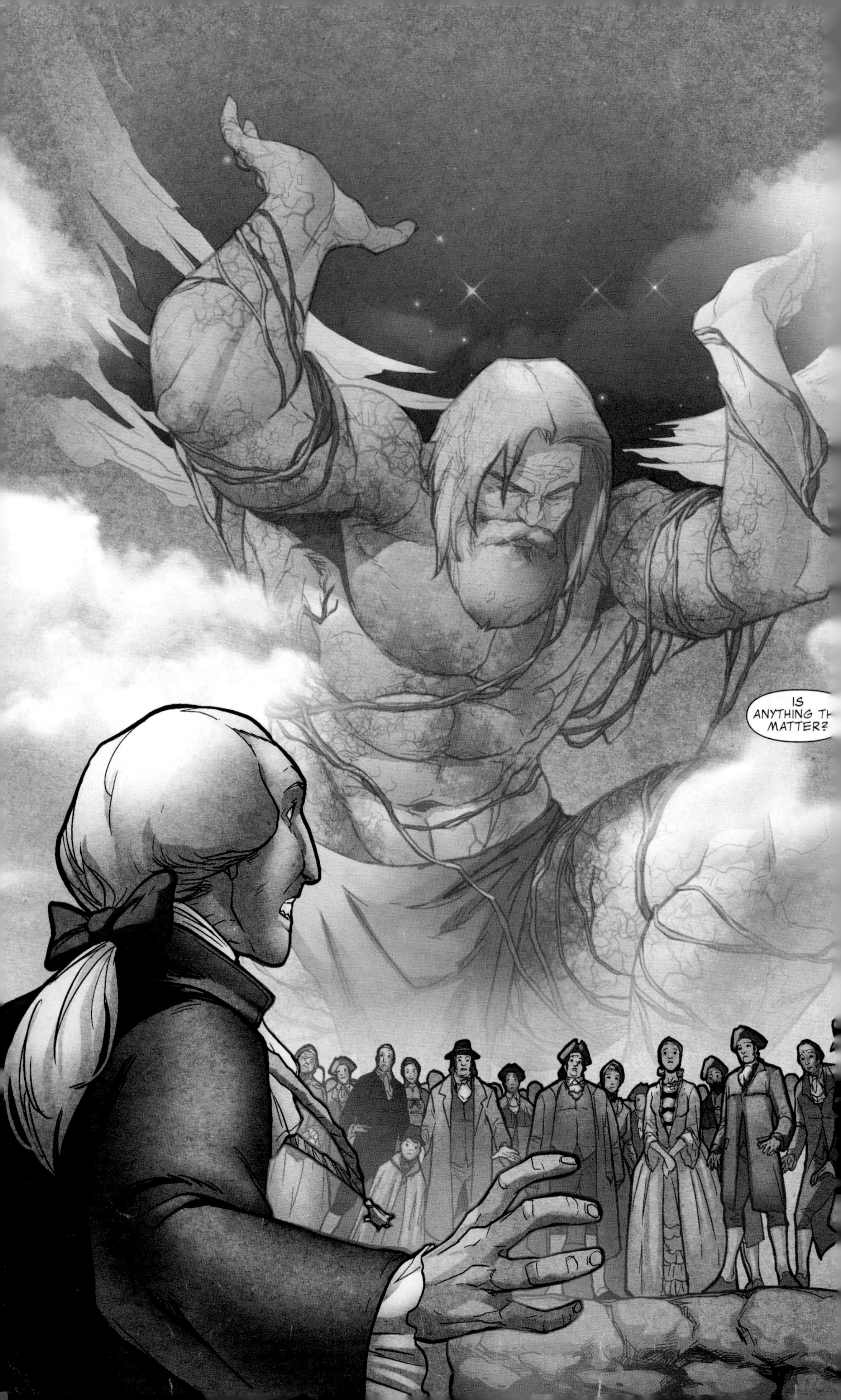
IS
ANYTHING TH
MATTER?

Shout-out Chorge Amadashington

## Second Inaugural ~~Address~~ of ~~George Washington~~

Amazonian Holding Cell, Flying Around

**P~~hiladelphia, Pennsylva~~nia**

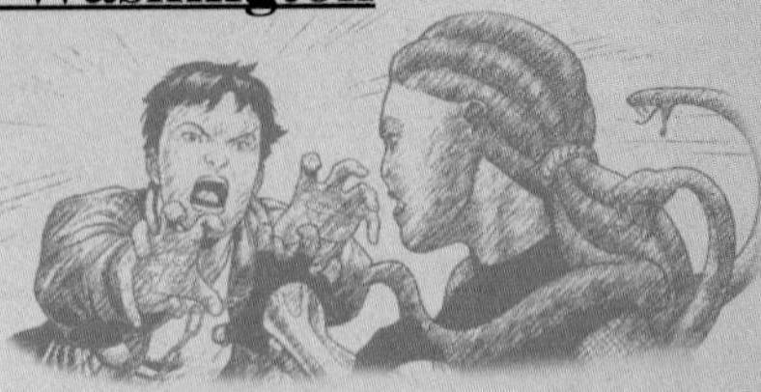

**Monday, March 4, 1793** or... now

Yo, people that aren't as smart as me,

~~Fellow Citizens~~,

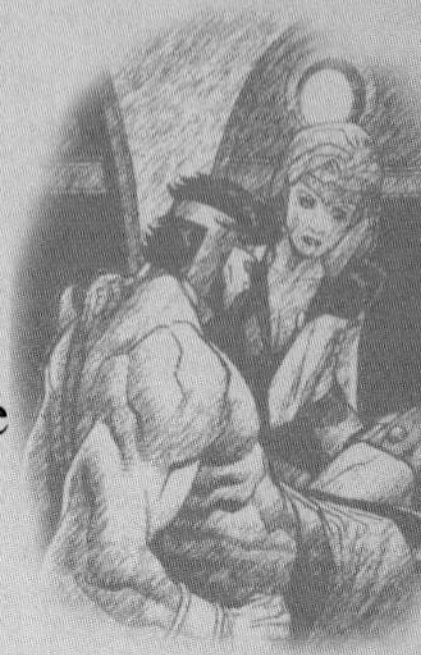

I am again ~~called upon by the voice of my country to~~ depending on my (maybe-dead) sidekick, Hercules, to save the day before Amazons execute ~~the functions of its Chief Magistrate~~ me.

When the ~~occasion proper for it~~ OMPHALOS (whatever that is) shall arrive, I shall endeavor to express the high sense I entertain of this distinguished honor, and of the confidence which has (even though my super-charged brain's fritzing due to lack of junk food) been reposed in me by the ~~people of united America~~ murder-happy chicks that've trapped me.

Previous to the execution of ~~any offical act of the President the Constitution requires an oath of office~~ the mega-HOT snaked-headed Delphyne, she wanted to rock the Amadeus. But Artume got her stab on.

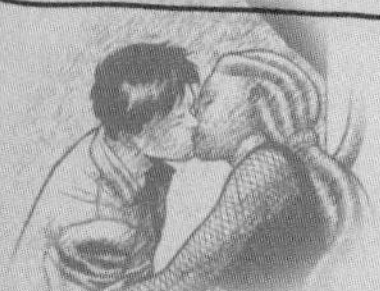

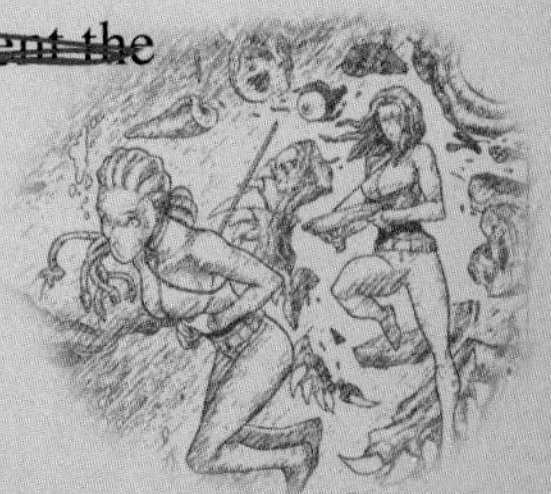

This Oath I am now about to take, and in your presence: That if it shall be found ~~during my administration of the Government I have in any instance violated willingly or knowingly the injunctions thereof~~ that the AmaZANYans don't need any more info from me, I may (besides incurring constitutional pubishment) be subject to ~~the upbraidings of all who are now witnesses of the present solemn ceremony~~ all sorts of unfun killing-related activities...

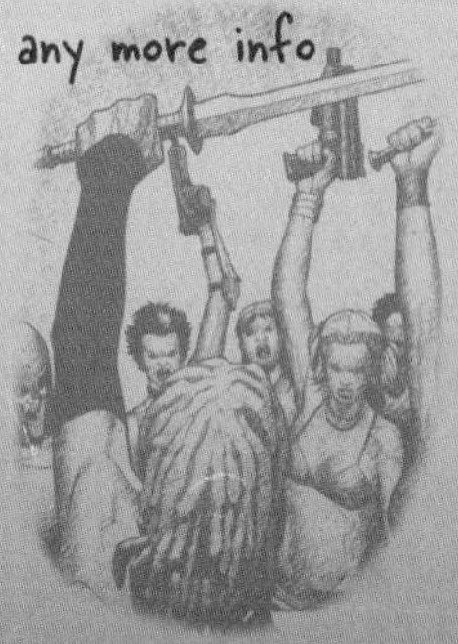

Yay adventure.

I want my puppy.

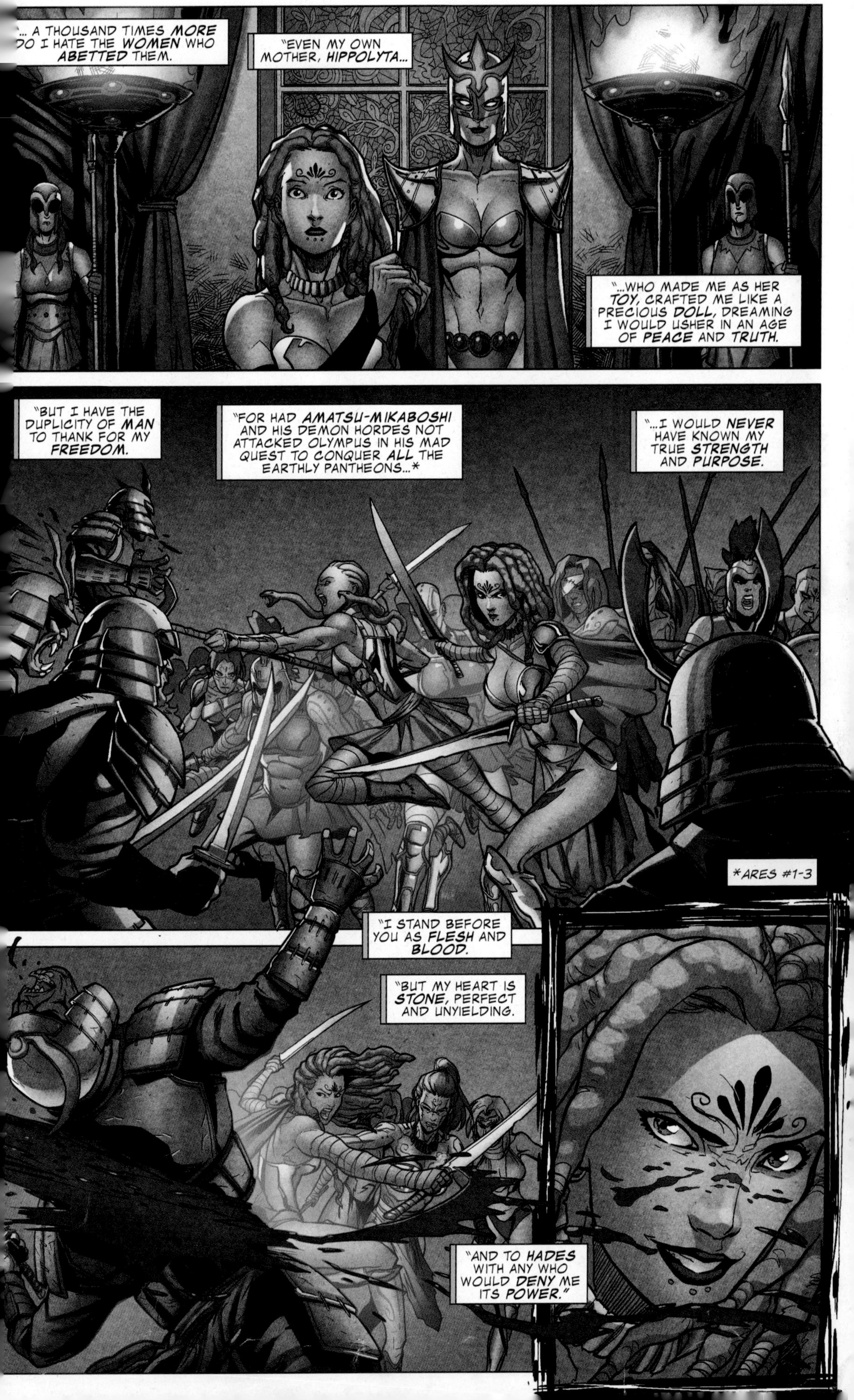
"... A THOUSAND TIMES MORE DO I HATE THE WOMEN WHO ABETTED THEM.
"EVEN MY OWN MOTHER, HIPPOLYTA...
"...WHO MADE ME AS HER TOY, CRAFTED ME LIKE A PRECIOUS DOLL, DREAMING I WOULD USHER IN AN AGE OF PEACE AND TRUTH.
"BUT I HAVE THE DUPLICITY OF MAN TO THANK FOR MY FREEDOM.
"FOR HAD AMATSU-MIKABOSHI AND HIS DEMON HORDES NOT ATTACKED OLYMPUS IN HIS MAD QUEST TO CONQUER ALL THE EARTHLY PANTHEONS...*
"...I WOULD NEVER HAVE KNOWN MY TRUE STRENGTH AND PURPOSE.
*ARES #1-3
"I STAND BEFORE YOU AS FLESH AND BLOOD.
"BUT MY HEART IS STONE, PERFECT AND UNYIELDING.
"AND TO HADES WITH ANY WHO WOULD DENY ME ITS POWER."

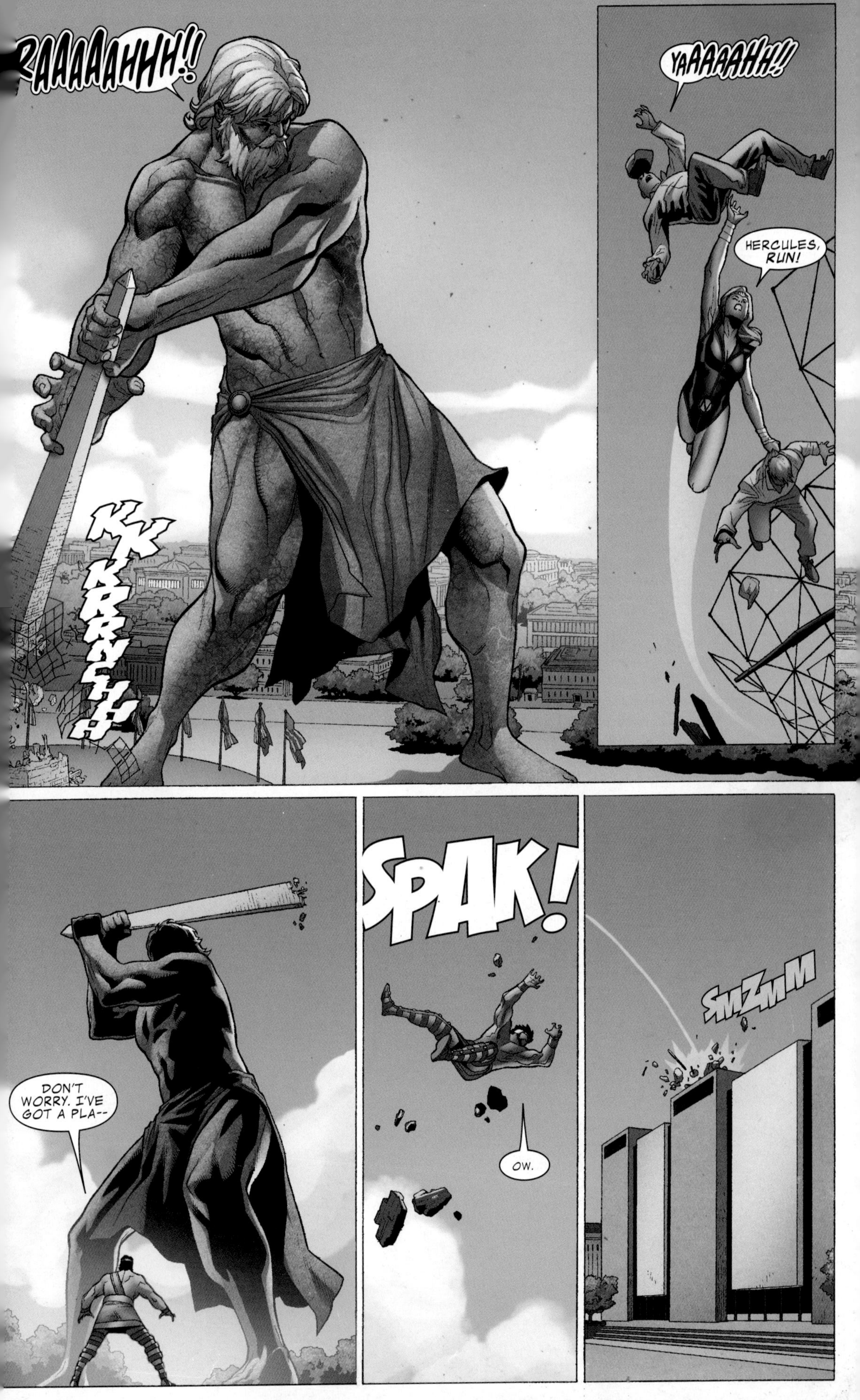
RAAAAAHHH!!
KKKRRNCH!!
YAAAAAHH!!
HERCULES, RUN!
DON'T WORRY. I'VE GOT A PLA--
SPAK!
OW.
SMZMM

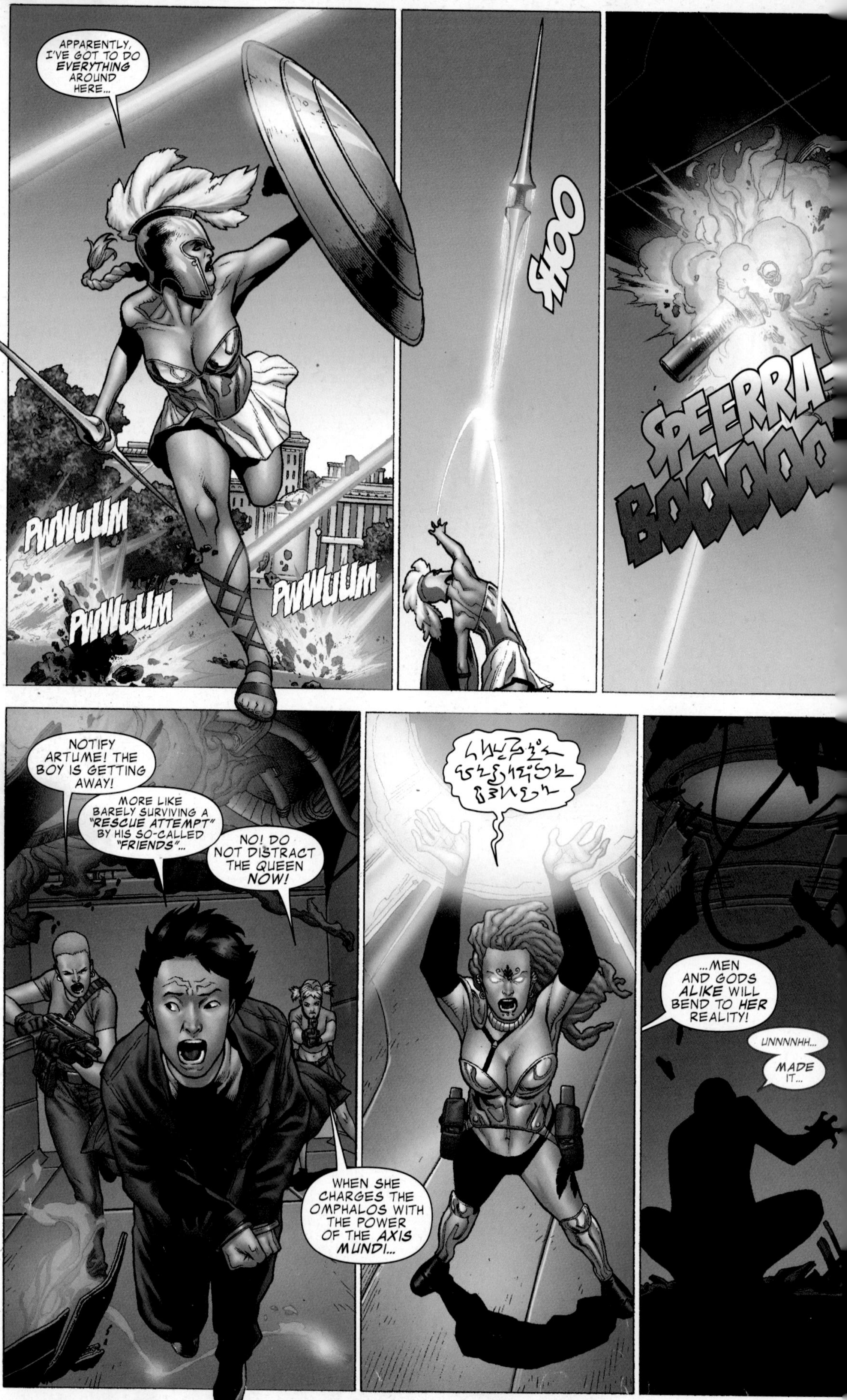
APPARENTLY, I'VE GOT TO DO EVERYTHING AROUND HERE...
PWUUM
PWUUM
PWUUM
SHOO
SPEERRA-BOOOOO
NOTIFY ARTUME! THE BOY IS GETTING AWAY!
MORE LIKE BARELY SURVIVING A "RESCUE ATTEMPT" BY HIS SO-CALLED "FRIENDS"...
NO! DO NOT DISTRACT THE QUEEN NOW!
WHEN SHE CHARGES THE OMPHALOS WITH THE POWER OF THE AXIS MUNDI...
...MEN AND GODS ALIKE WILL BEND TO HER REALITY!
UNNNNHH...
MADE IT...

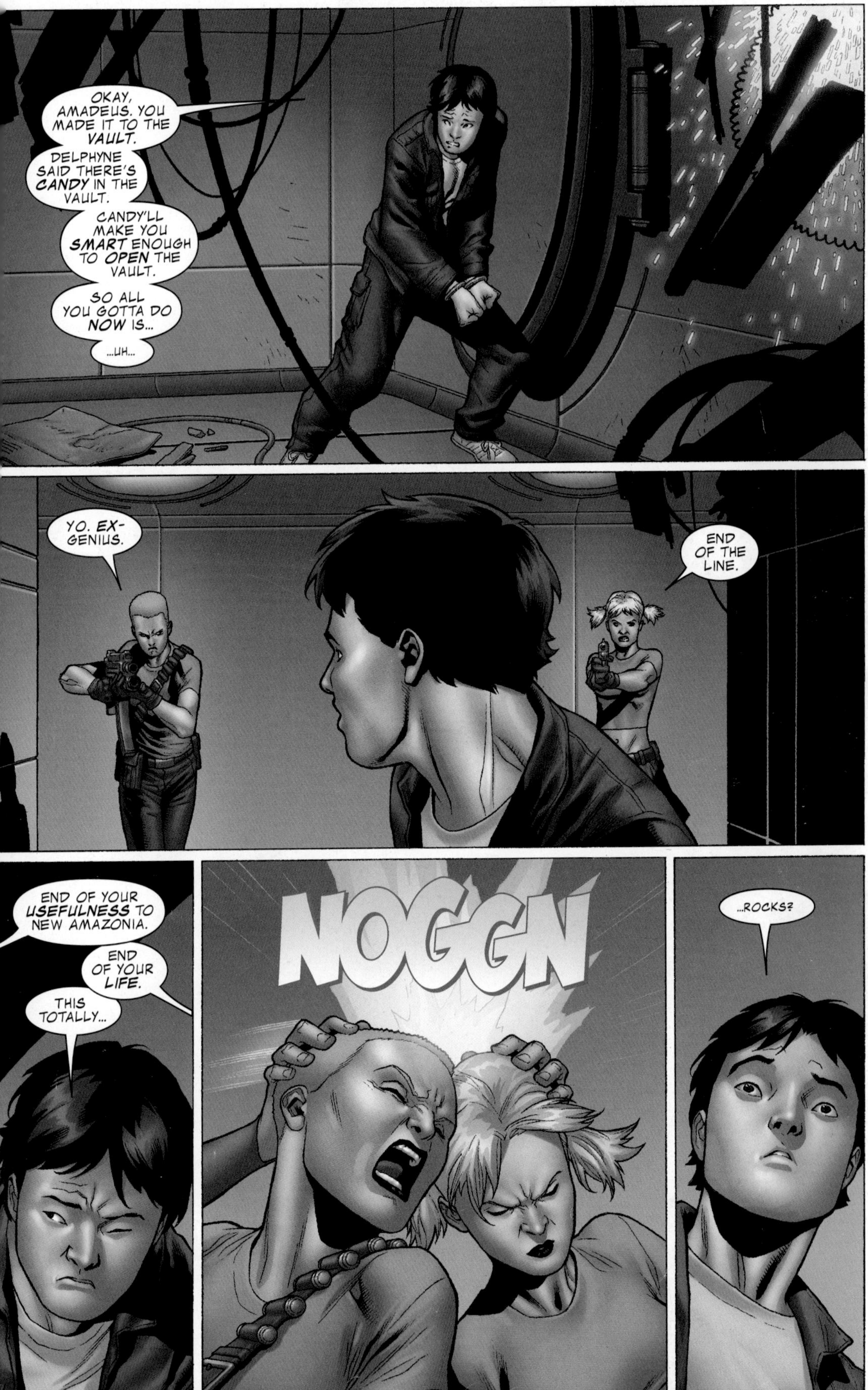
OKAY, AMADEUS. YOU MADE IT TO THE VAULT.
DELPHYNE SAID THERE'S CANDY IN THE VAULT.
CANDY'LL MAKE YOU SMART ENOUGH TO OPEN THE VAULT.
SO ALL YOU GOTTA DO NOW IS...
...UH...
YO. EX-GENIUS.
END OF THE LINE.
END OF YOUR USEFULNESS TO NEW AMAZONIA.
END OF YOUR LIFE.
THIS TOTALLY...
NOGGN
...ROCKS?

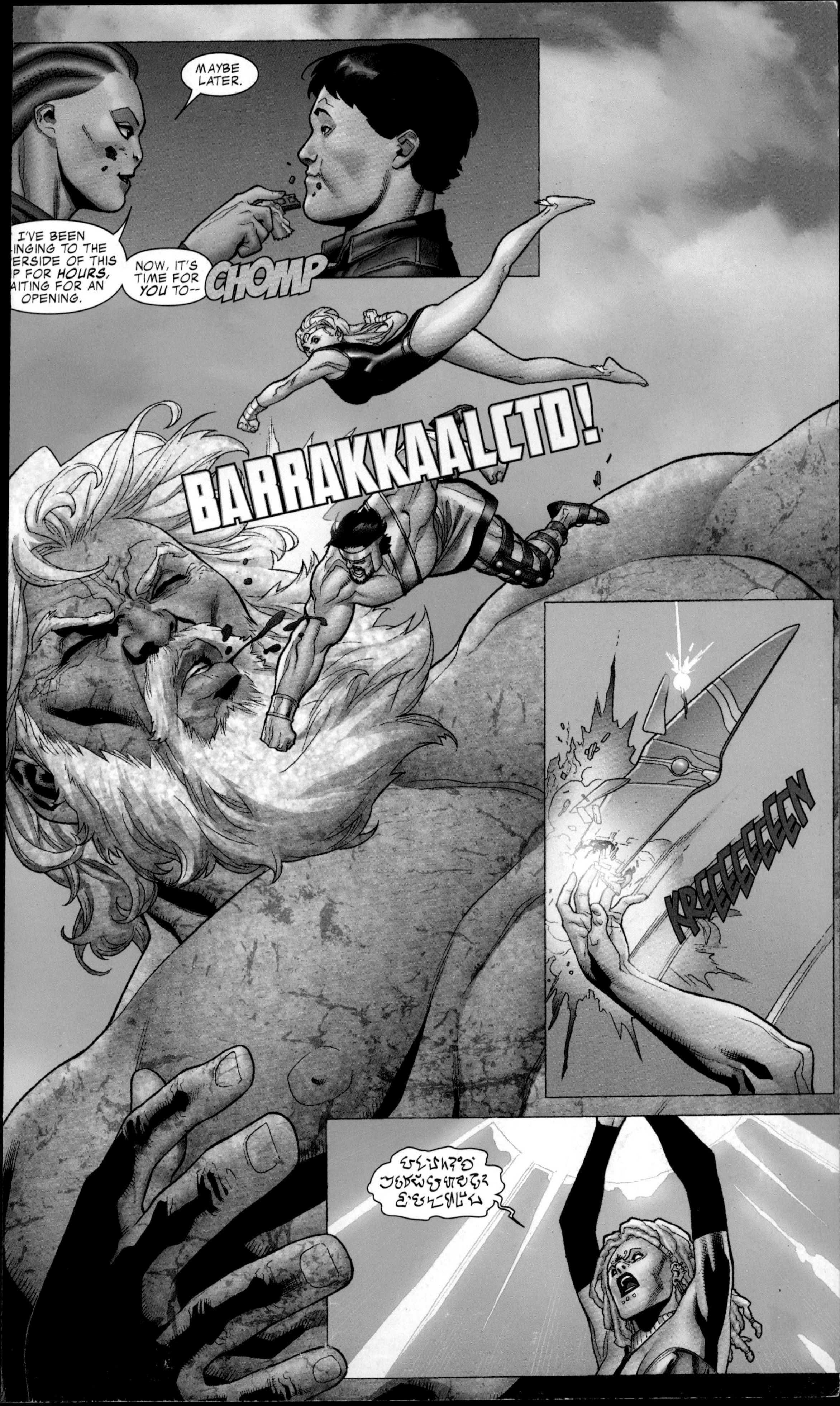
MAYBE LATER.
I'VE BEEN -INGING TO THE -ERSIDE OF THIS -P FOR HOURS, -AITING FOR AN OPENING.
NOW, IT'S TIME FOR YOU TO--
CHOMP
BARRAKKAALCTO!
KREEEEEEEN

UKK!

WHACK!

NOW--LET AMAZONIA RULE TODAY, YESTERDAY, AND FOREVER!

SMACK!

AAAH!

OH, NO.

OH...

...YES.

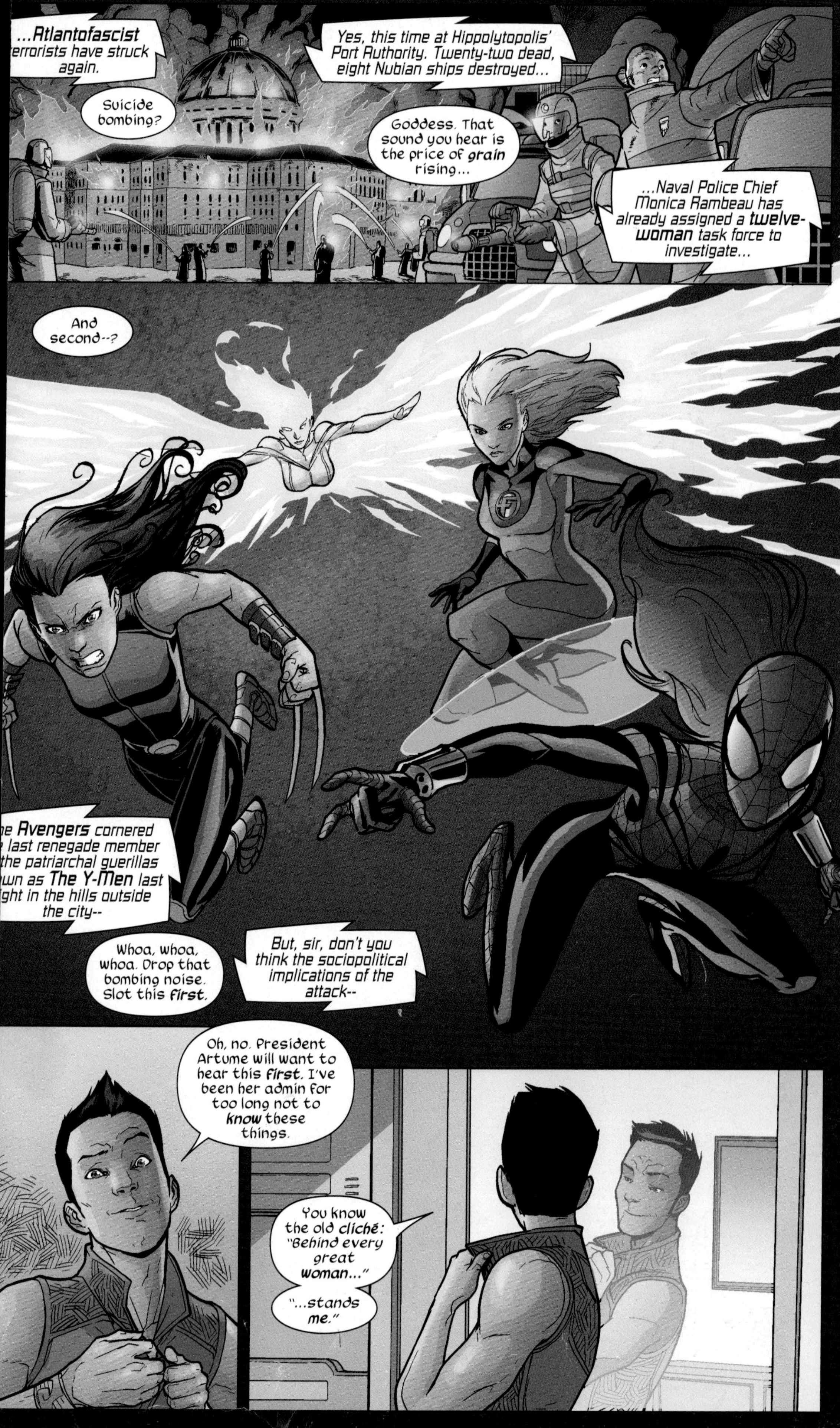
...Atlantofascist errorists have struck again.
Suicide bombing?
Yes, this time at Hippolytopolis' Port Authority. Twenty-two dead, eight Nubian ships destroyed...
Goddess. That sound you hear is the price of grain rising...
...Naval Police Chief Monica Rambeau has already assigned a twelve-woman task force to investigate...
And second--?
he Avengers cornered last renegade member the patriarchal guerillas wn as The Y-Men last ght in the hills outside the city--
Whoa, whoa, whoa. Drop that bombing noise. Slot this first.
But, sir, don't you think the sociopolitical implications of the attack--
Oh, no. President Artume will want to hear this first. I've been her admin for too long not to know these things.
You know the old cliché: "Behind every great woman..."
"...stands me."

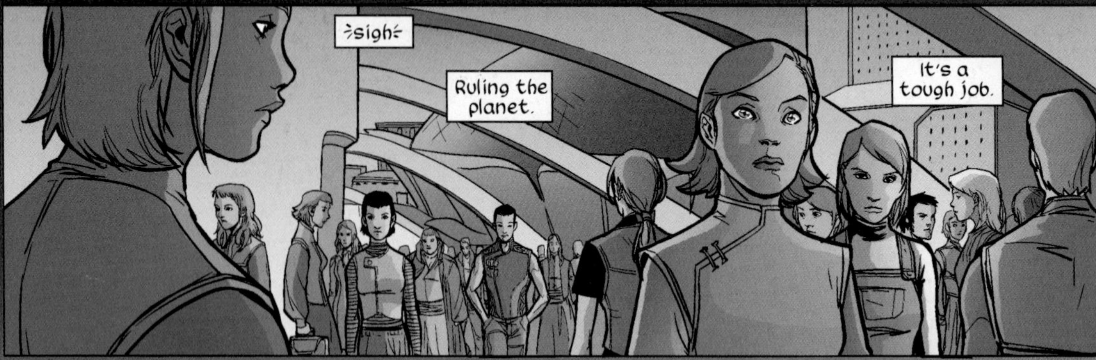

-sigh-
Ruling the planet.
It's a tough job.


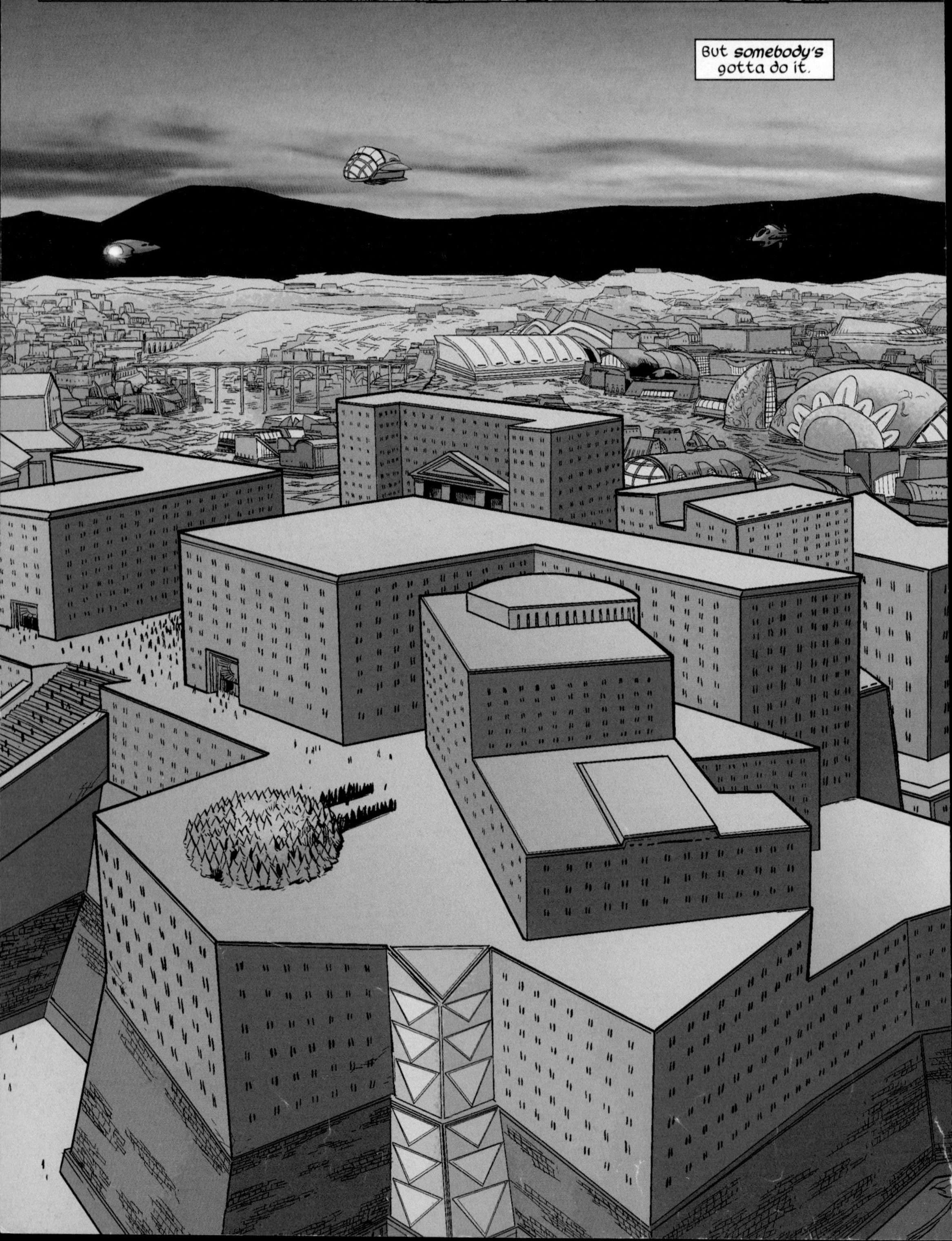

But *somebody's* gotta do it.

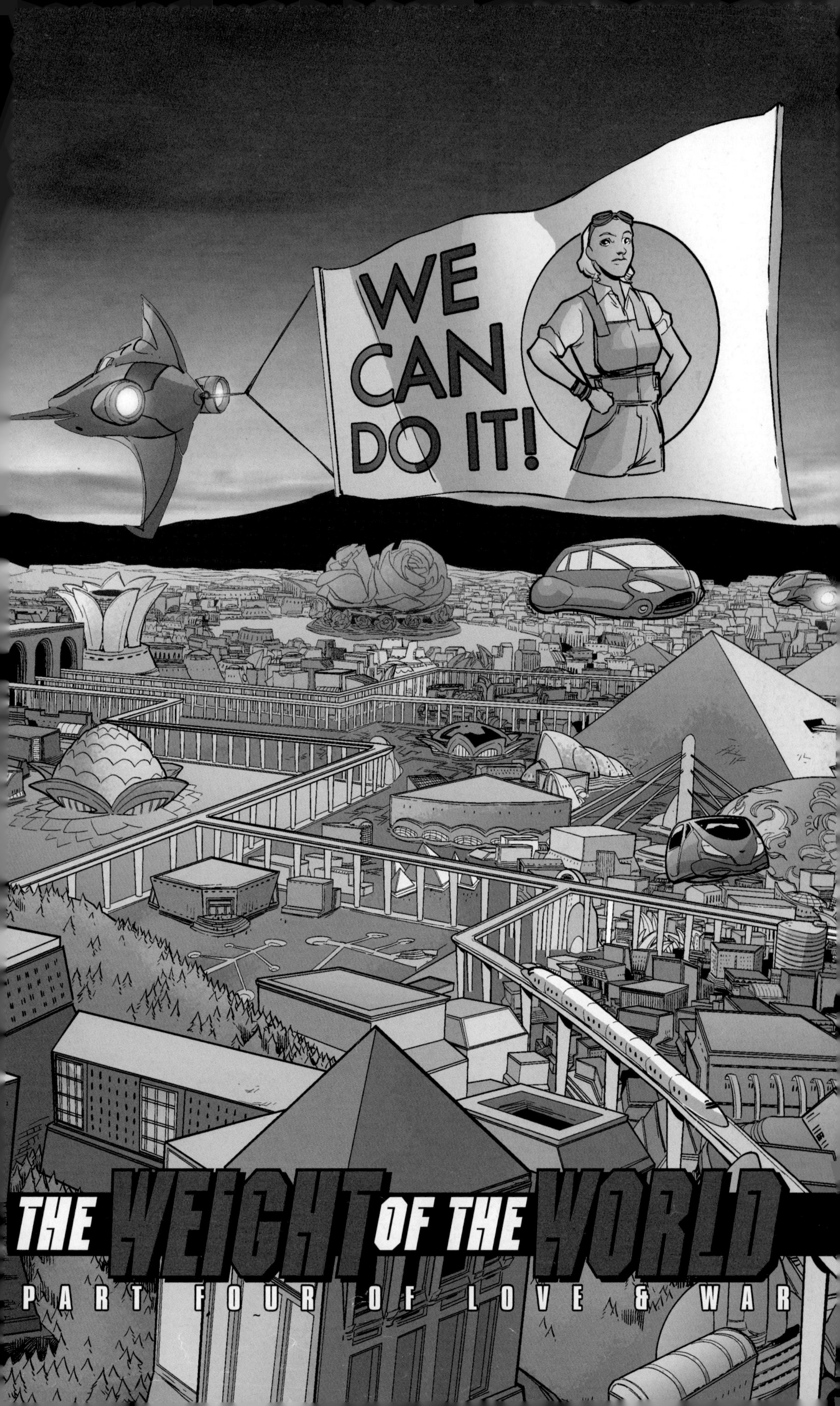

WE CAN DO IT!
THE WEIGHT OF THE WORLD
PART FOUR OF LOVE & WAR

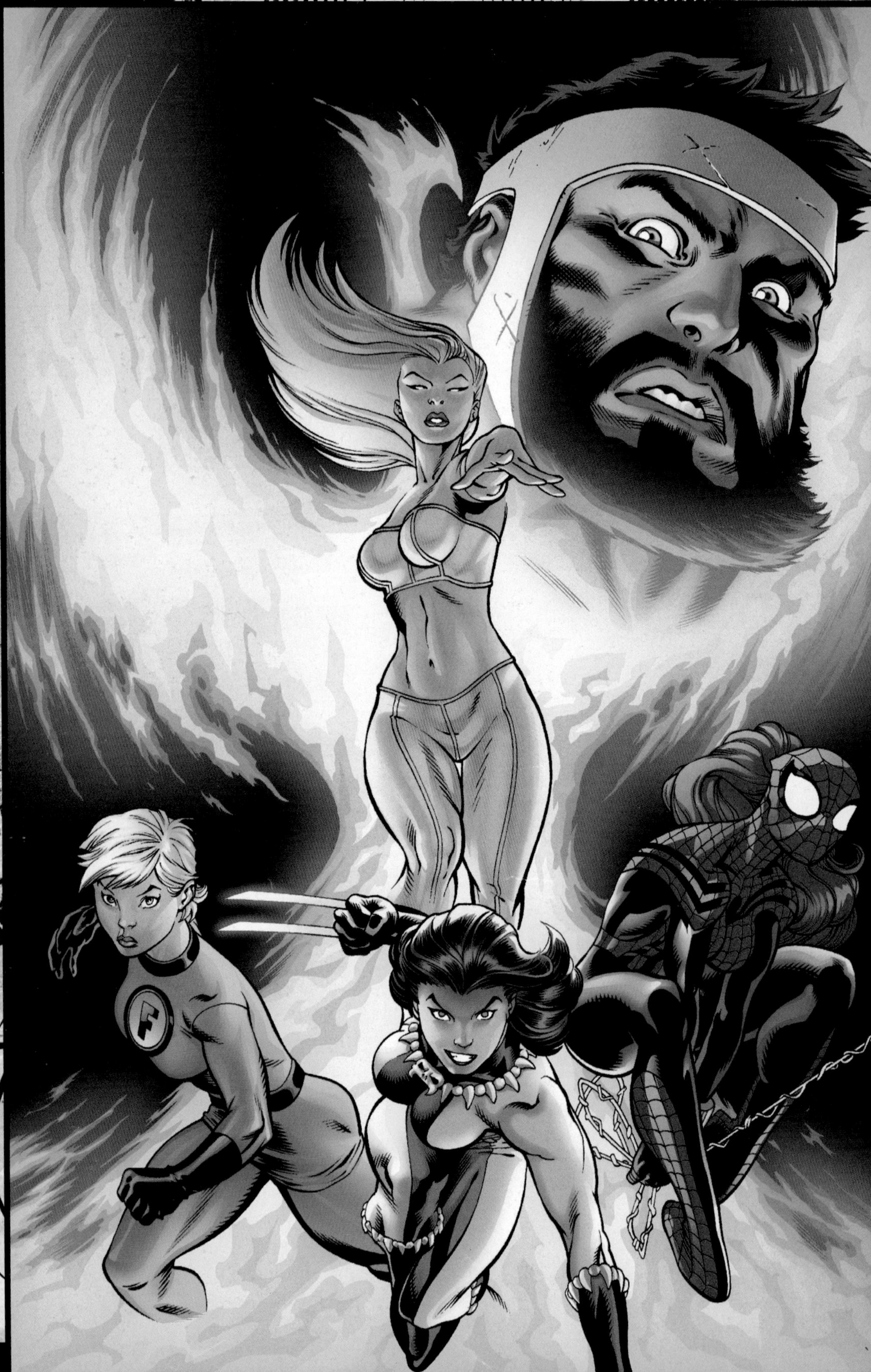

INCREDIBLE HERCULES #125

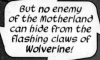

But no enemy of the Motherland can hide from the flashing claws of **Wolverine!**

And your friendly neighborhood **Spider-Woman** wrapped him up in a neat ball for delivery to The Culling Center!

So, though **one** threat to hearth and home has been successfully repelled...

...remember, laddies and gentlewomen--between terrorist **Y-Men** and **Atlanteans** who hate our freedom--

--your family and nation are under **constant** attack. Stay **vigilant.**

I can't watch all of you at **once...**

...as much as I'd **like** to!

This is **President Artume,** hoping you own your day, U.S.A.!

CREATE

NURTURE PROTECT

"**Your Morn-Brief with Madame President**" is a production of the Amazonian Secretariat of Edutainment...

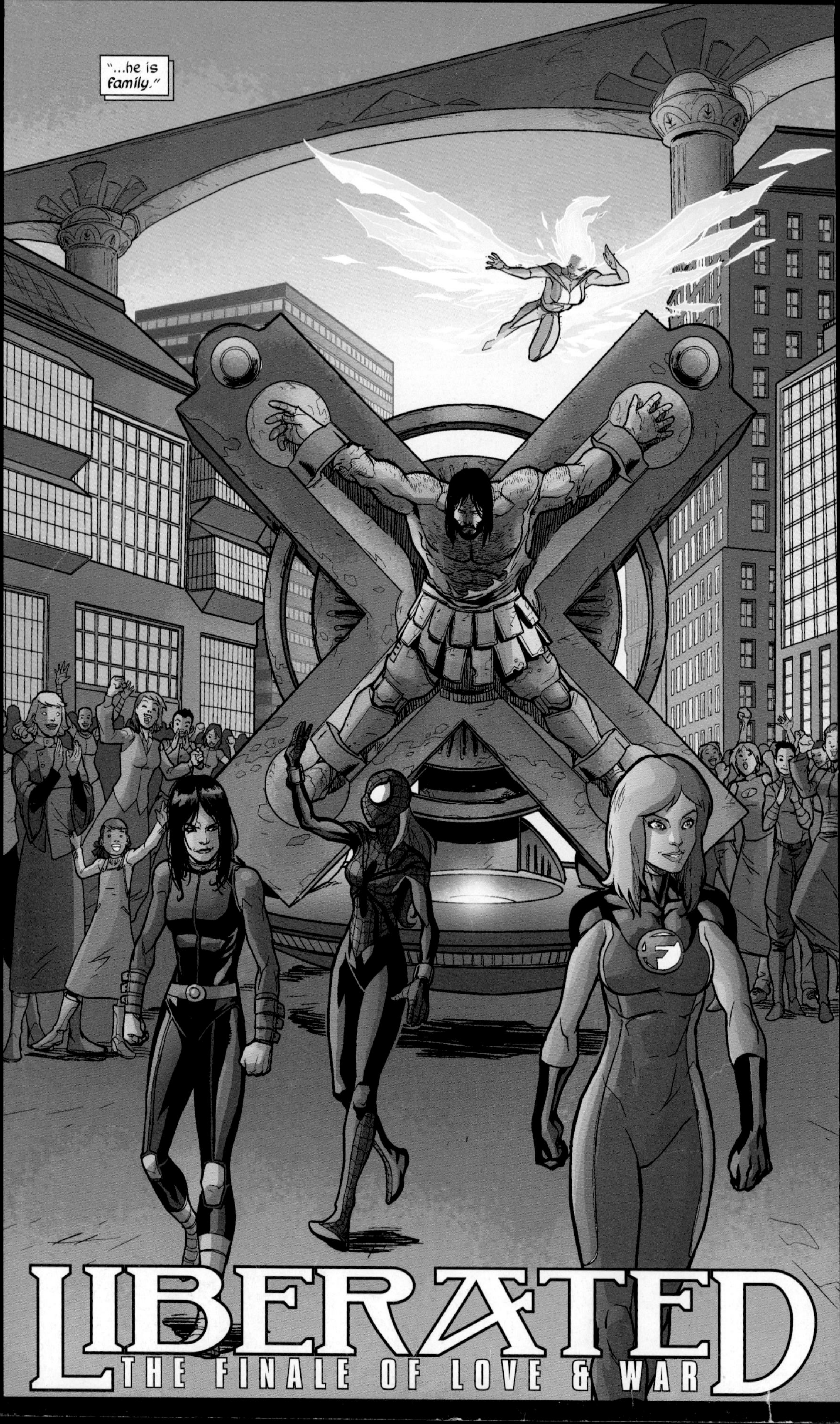
"...he is family."
LIBERATED
THE FINALE OF LOVE & WAR

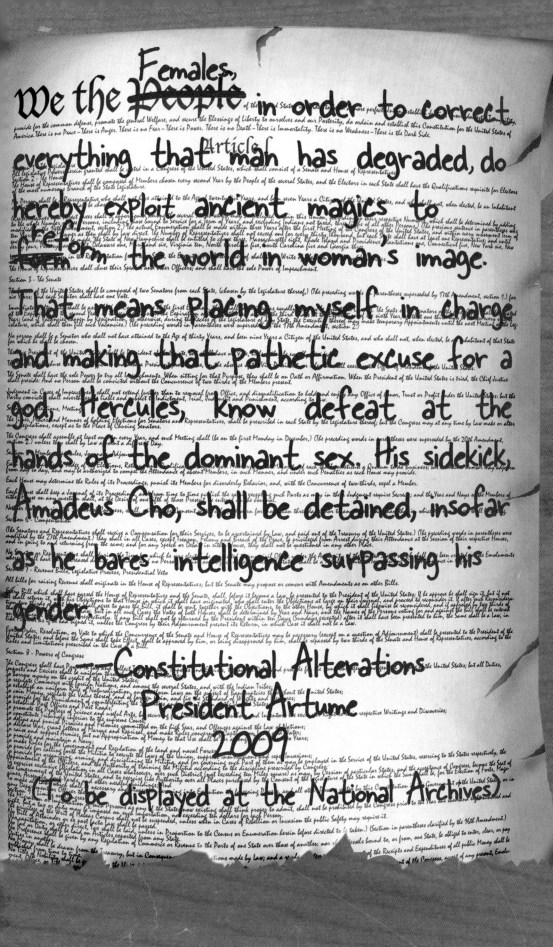

We the ~~People~~ Females, in order to correct everything that man has degraded, do hereby exploit ancient magics to ~~form~~ reform the world in woman's image. That means placing myself in charge and making that pathetic excuse for a god, Hercules, know defeat at the hands of the dominant sex. His sidekick, Amadeus Cho, shall be detained, insofar as he bares intelligence surpassing his gender.

—Constitutional Alterations
President Artume
2009
(To be displayed at the National Archives)

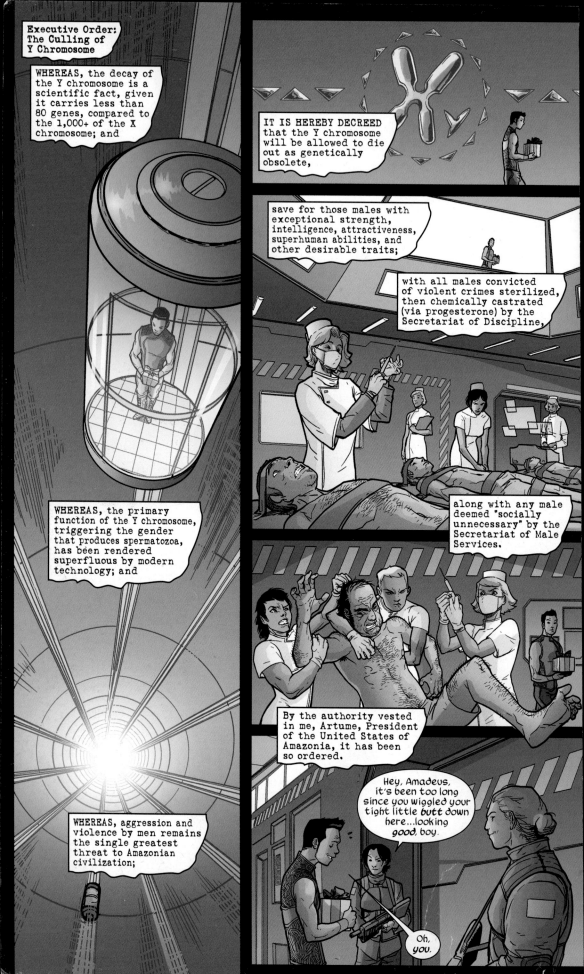

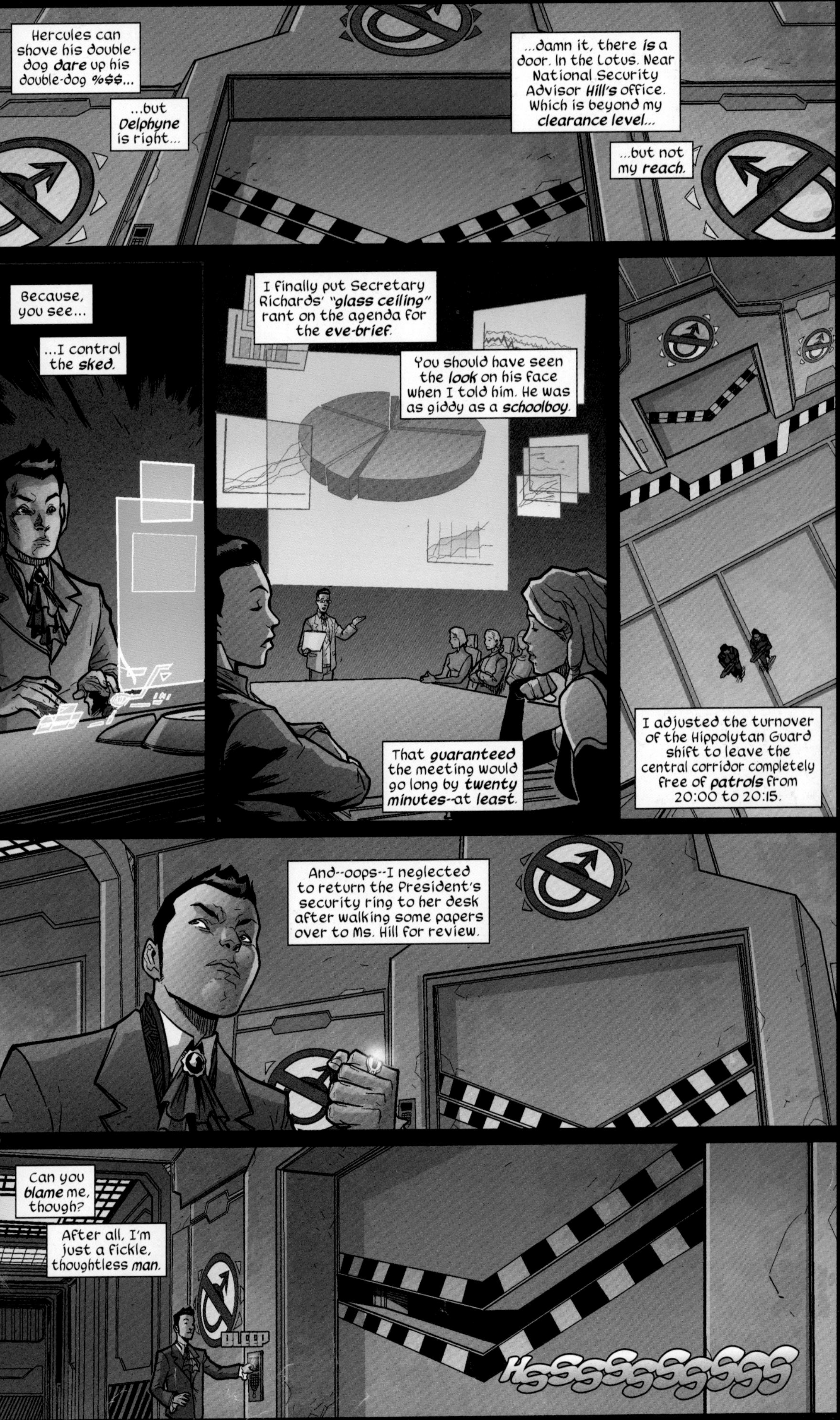
Hercules can shove his double-dog dare up his double-dog %$$...
...but Delphyne is right...
...damn it, there is a door. In the Lotus. Near National Security Advisor Hill's office. Which is beyond my clearance level...
...but not my reach.
Because, you see...
...I control the sked.
I finally put Secretary Richards' "glass ceiling" rant on the agenda for the eve-brief.
You should have seen the look on his face when I told him. He was as giddy as a schoolboy.
That guaranteed the meeting would go long by twenty minutes--at least.
I adjusted the turnover of the Hippolytan Guard shift to leave the central corridor completely free of patrols from 20:00 to 20:15.
And--oops--I neglected to return the President's security ring to her desk after walking some papers over to Ms. Hill for review.
Can you blame me, though?
After all, I'm just a fickle, thoughtless man.
BLEEP
HSSSSSSSSSSS

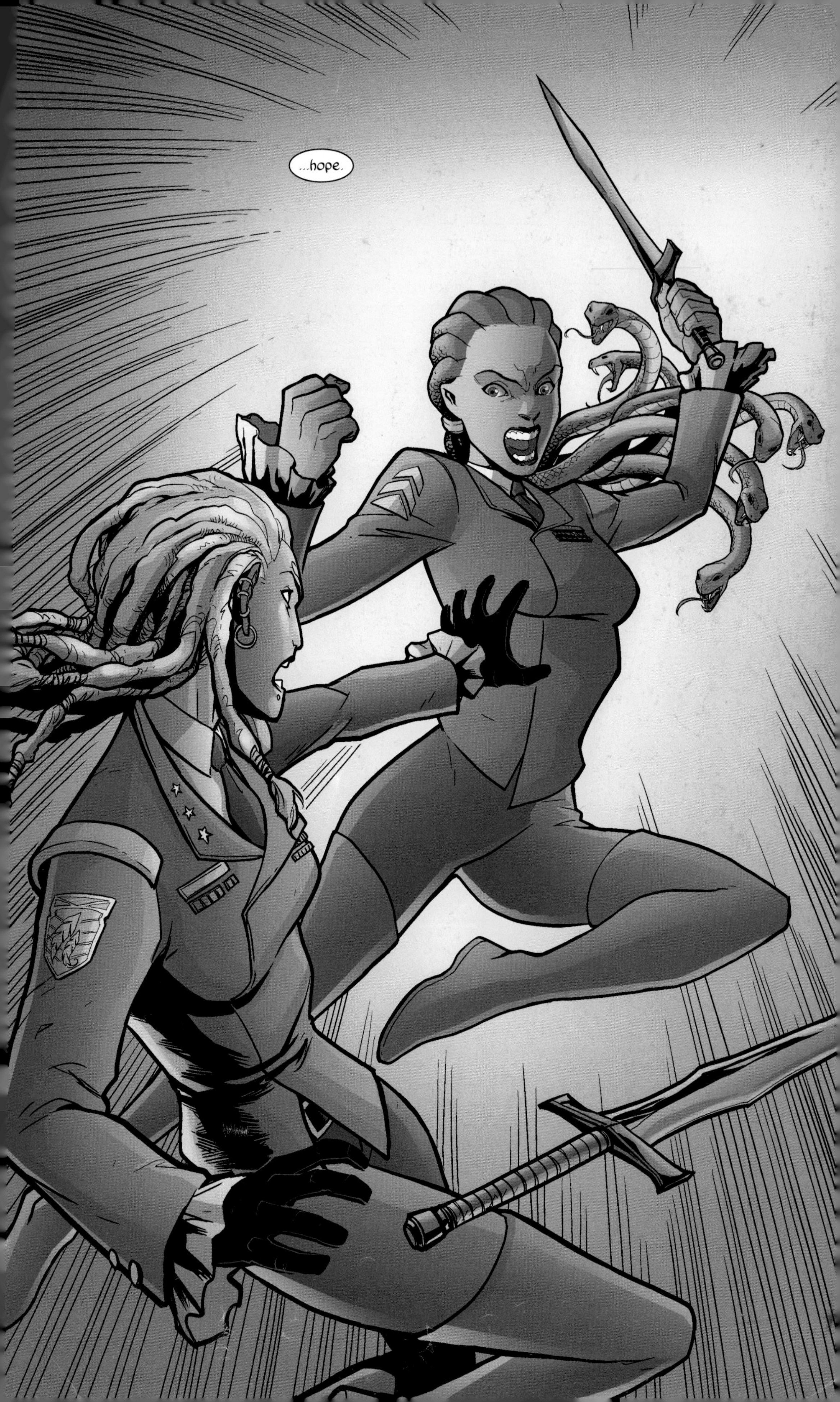
...hope.

**NEXT:**
**THE ORIGIN OF HERCULES AND THE SEARCH FOR KIRBY!**

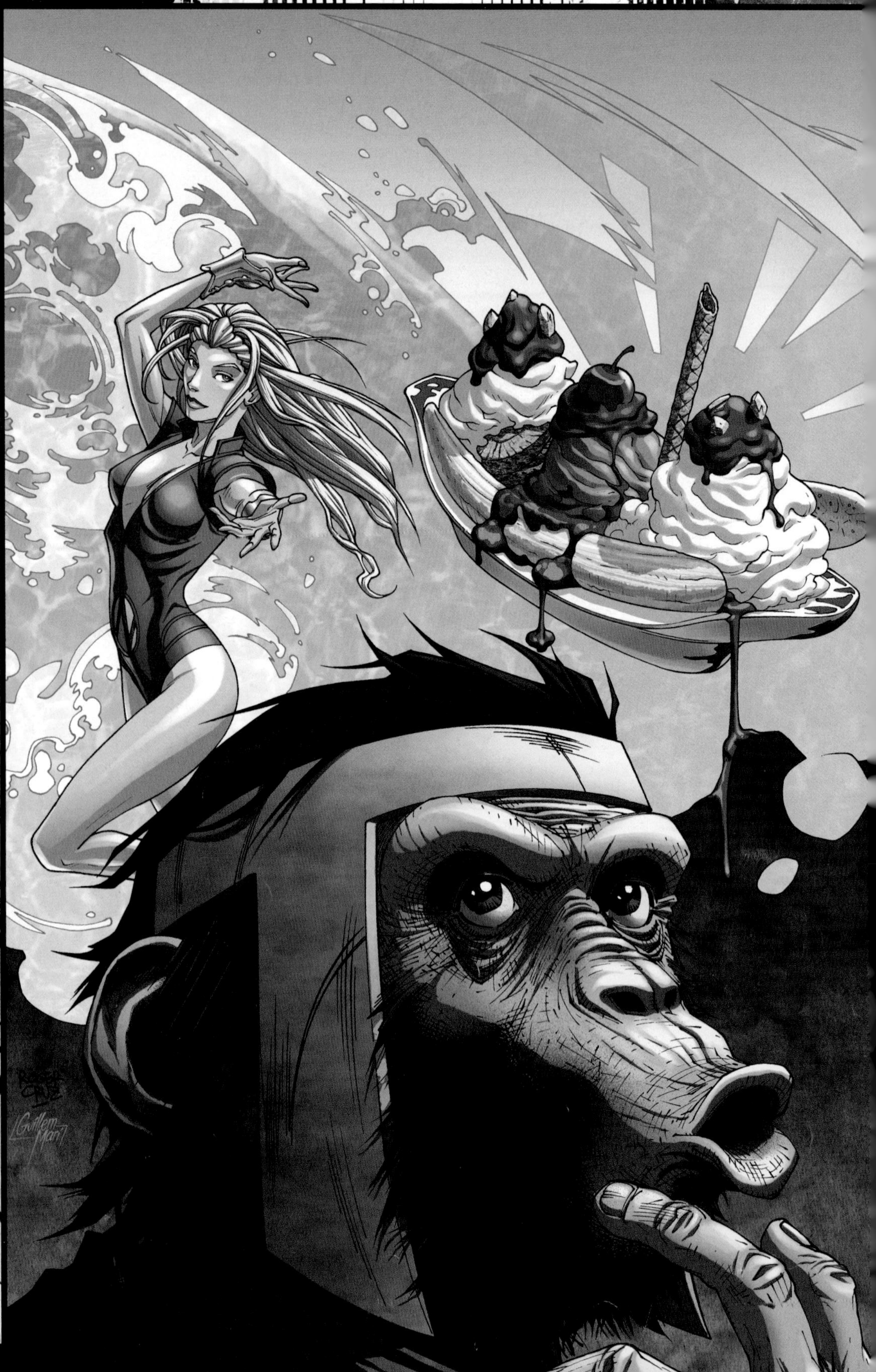

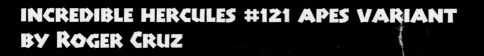

INCREDIBLE HERCULES #121 APES VARIANT
BY ROGER CRUZ

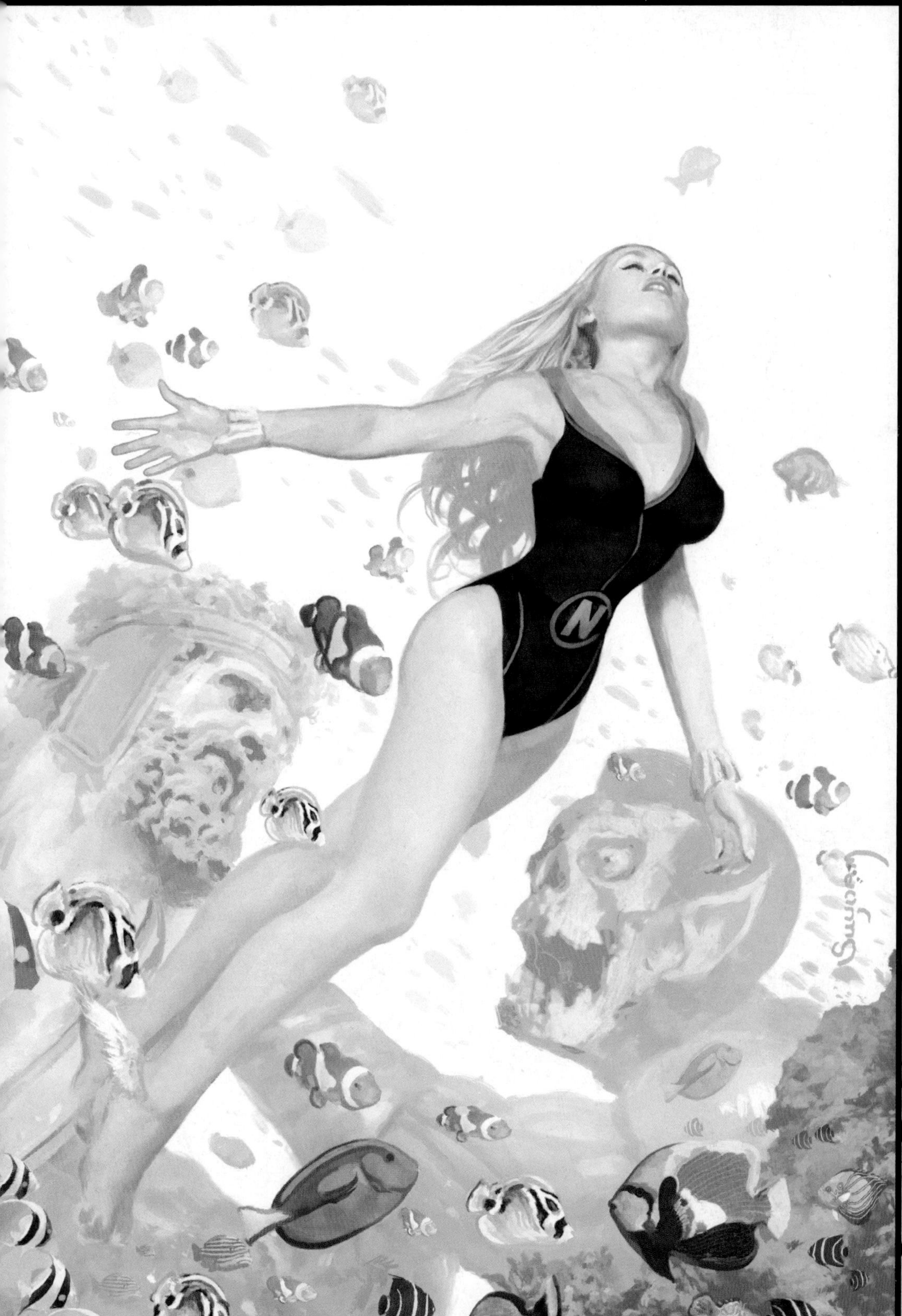

**INCREDIBLE HERCULES #122 ZOMBIE VARIANT**
**BY ARTHUR SUYDAM**

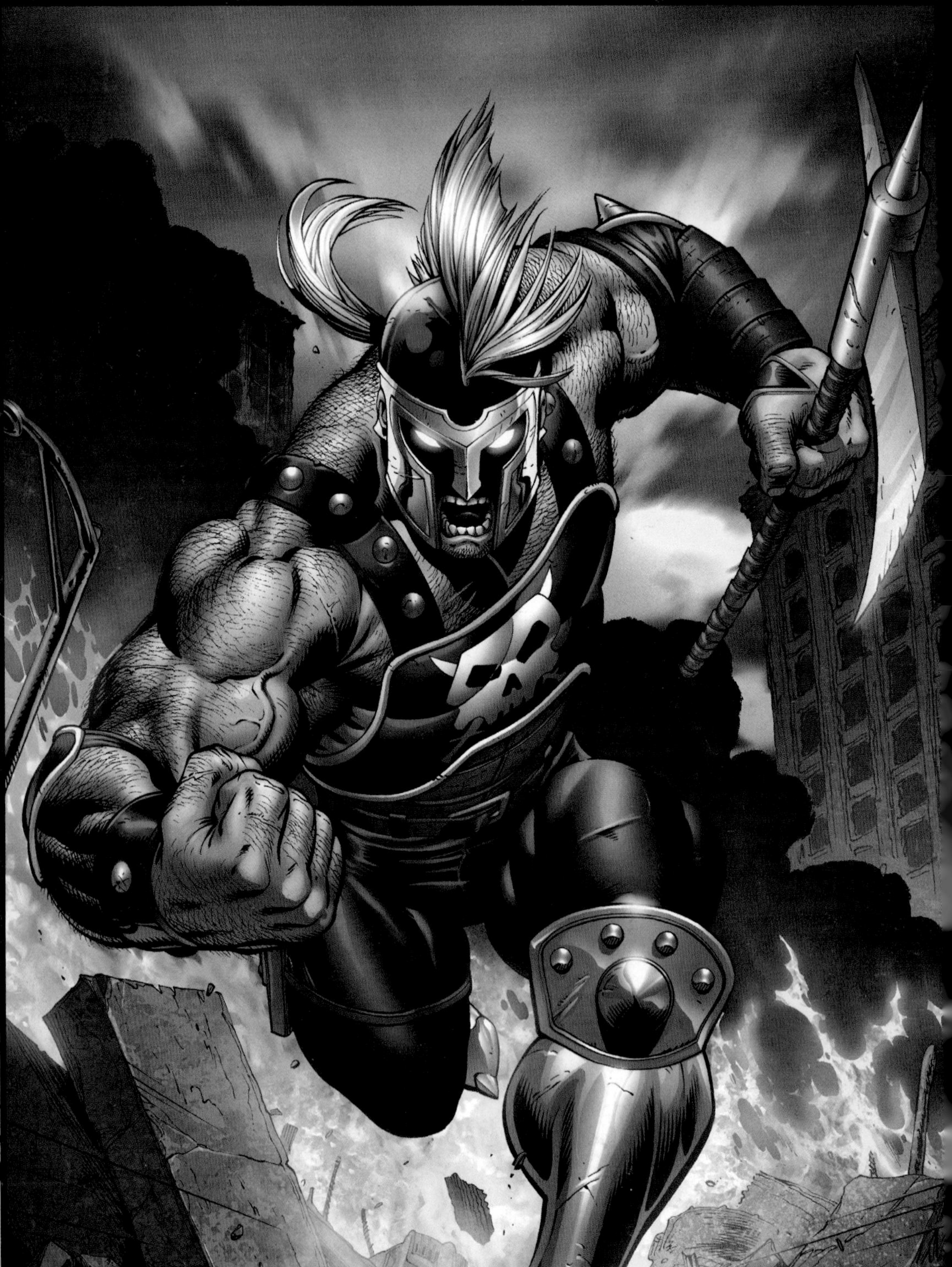

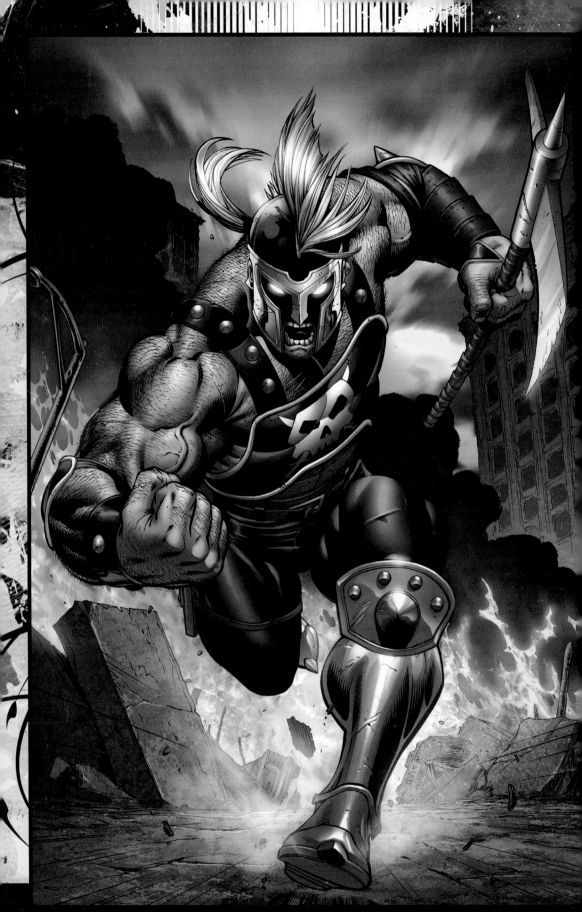

INCREDIBLE HERCULES #124 VARIANT
BY ED MCGUINNESS

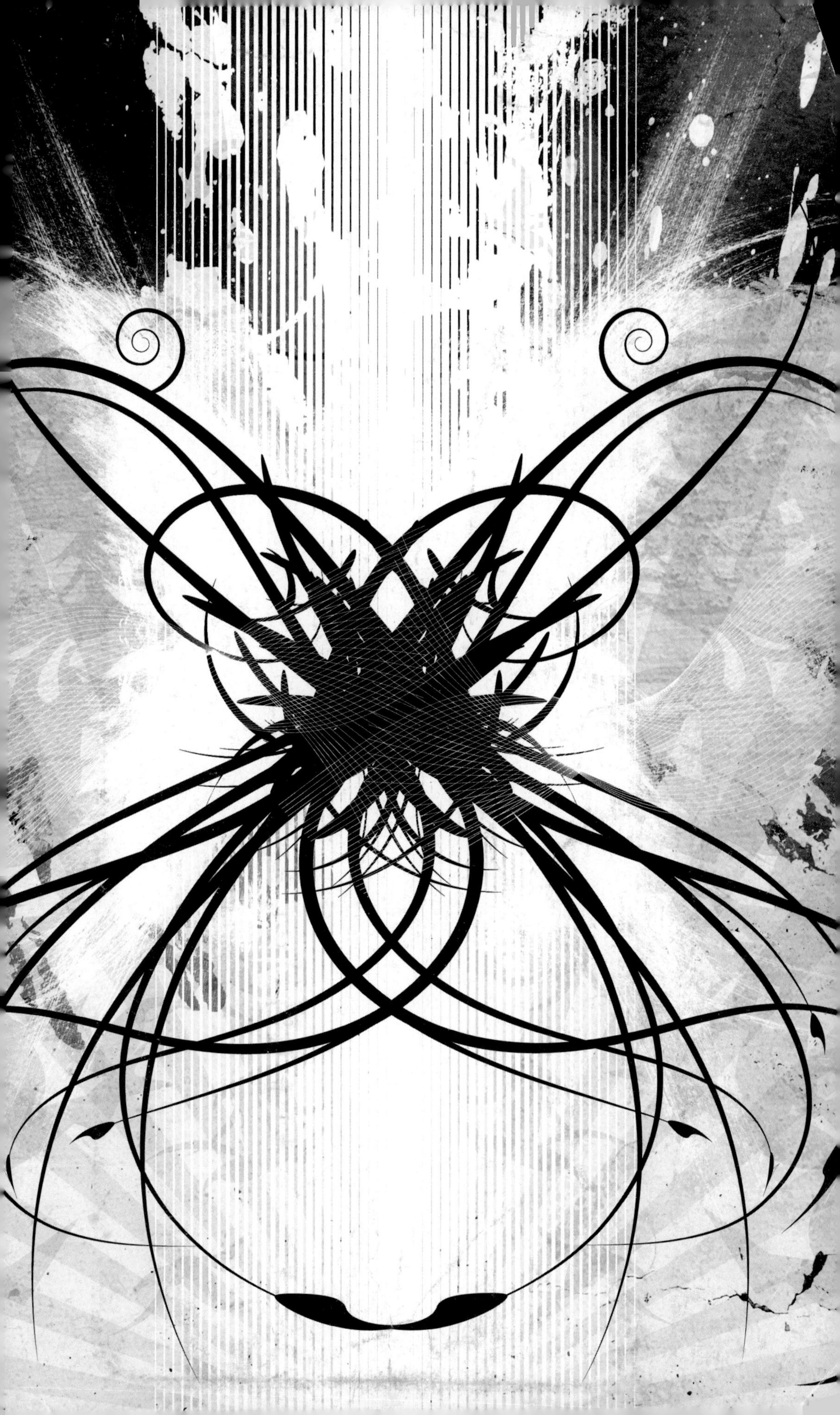

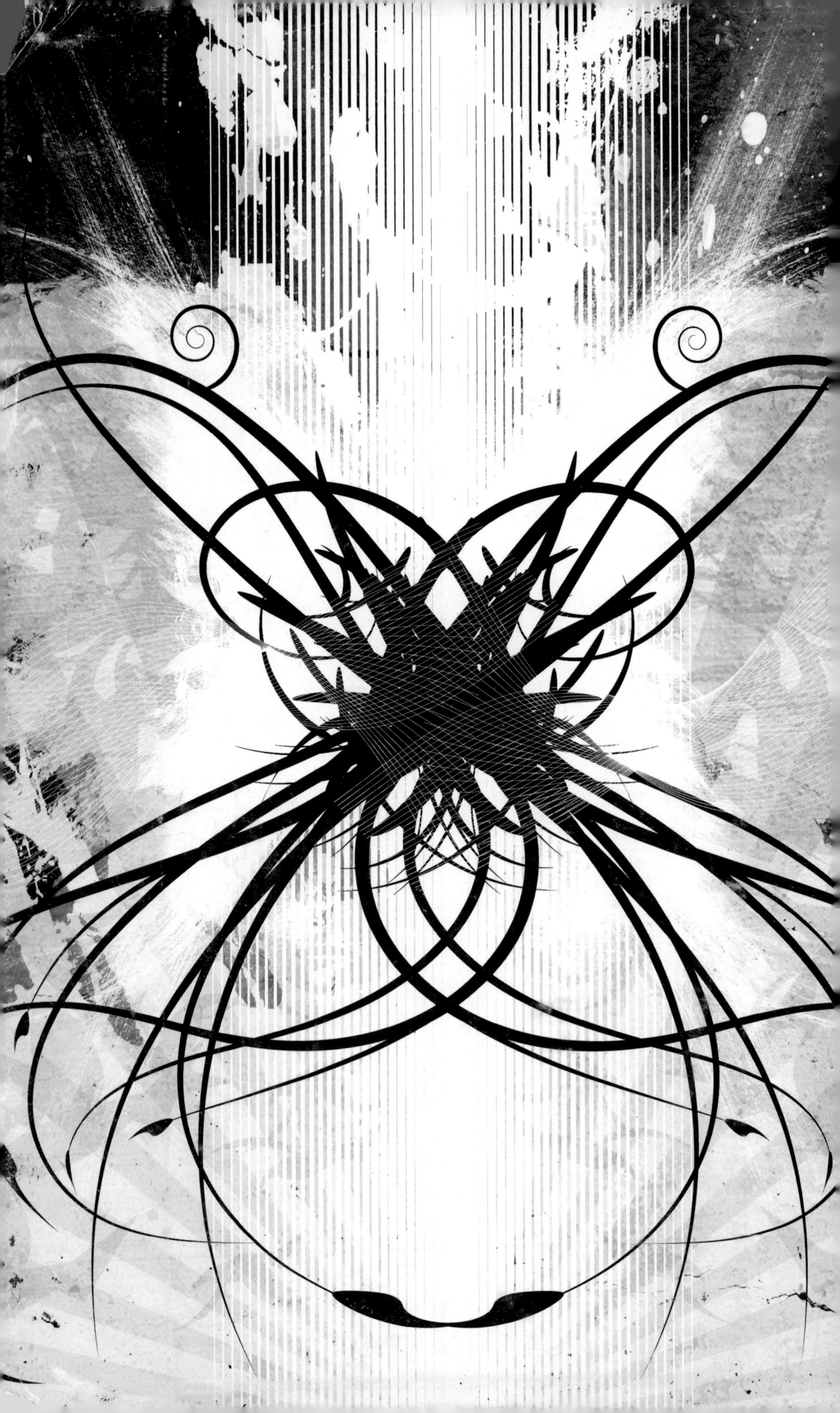